An Analysis of

Thucydides's

History of the
Peloponnesian War

Mark Fisher

Published by Macat International Ltd
24:13 Coda Centre, 189 Munster Road, London SW6 6AW.

Distributed exclusively by Routledge
2 Park Square, Milton Park, Abingdon, Oxon OX14 4RN
711 Third Avenue, New York, NY 10017, USA

Routledge is an imprint of the Taylor & Francis Group, an informa business

www.macat.com
info@macat.com

Cataloguing in Publication Data
A catalogue record for this book is available from the British Library.
Library of Congress Cataloguing-in-Publication Data is available upon request.
Cover illustration: Etienne Gilfillan

ISBN 978-1-912303-49-6 (hardback)
ISBN 978-1-912127-89-4 (paperback)
ISBN 978-1-912282-37-1 (e-book)

Notice
The information in this book is designed to orientate readers of the work under analysis,
to elucidate and contextualise its key ideas and themes, and to aid in the development
of critical thinking skills. It is not meant to be used, nor should it be used, as a
substitute for original thinking or in place of original writing or research. References and
notes are provided for informational purposes and their presence does not constitute
endorsement of the information or opinions therein. This book is presented solely for
educational purposes. It is sold on the understanding that the publisher is not engaged
to provide any scholarly advice. The publisher has made every effort to ensure that
this book is accurate and up-to-date, but makes no warranties or representations with
regard to the completeness or reliability of the information it contains. The information
and the opinions provided herein are not guaranteed or warranted to produce particular
results and may not be suitable for students of every ability. The publisher shall not be
liable for any loss, damage or disruption arising from any errors or omissions, or from
the use of this book, including, but not limited to, special, incidental, consequential or
other damages caused, or alleged to have been caused, directly or indirectly, by the
information contained within.

CONTENTS

THE MACAT LIBRARY

The Macat Library is a series of unique academic explorations of seminal works in the humanities and social sciences – books and papers that have had a significant and widely recognised impact on their disciplines. It has been created to serve as much more than just a summary of what lies between the covers of a great book. It illuminates and explores the influences on, ideas of, and impact of that book. Our goal is to offer a learning resource that encourages critical thinking and fosters a better, deeper understanding of important ideas.

Each publication is divided into three Sections: Influences, Ideas, and Impact. Each Section has four Modules. These explore every important facet of the work, and the responses to it.

This Section-Module structure makes a Macat Library book easy to use, but it has another important feature. Because each Macat book is written to the same format, it is possible (and encouraged!) to cross-reference multiple Macat books along the same lines of inquiry or research. This allows the reader to open up interesting interdisciplinary pathways.

To further aid your reading, lists of glossary terms and people mentioned are included at the end of this book (these are indicated by an asterisk [*] throughout) – as well as a list of works cited.

Macat has worked with the University of Cambridge to identify the elements of critical thinking and understand the ways in which six different skills combine to enable effective thinking.
Three allow us to fully understand a problem; three more give us the tools to solve it. Together, these six skills make up the **PACIER** model of critical thinking. They are:

ANALYSIS – understanding how an argument is built
EVALUATION – exploring the strengths and weaknesses of an argument
INTERPRETATION – understanding issues of meaning

CREATIVE THINKING – coming up with new ideas and fresh connections
PROBLEM-SOLVING – producing strong solutions
REASONING – creating strong arguments

To find out more, visit **WWW.MACAT.COM.**

CRITICAL THINKING AND *THE HISTORY OF THE PELOPONNESIAN WAR*

Primary critical thinking skill: ANALYSIS
Secondary critical thinking skill: REASONING

Few works can claim to form the foundation stones of one entire academic discipline, let alone two, but Thucydides's celebrated *History of the Peloponnesian War* is not only one of the first great works of history, but also the departure point from which the modern discipline of international relations has been built. This is the case largely because the author is a master of analysis; setting out with the aim of giving a clear, well-reasoned account of one of the seminal events of the age – a war that resulted in the collapse of Athenian power and the rise of Sparta – Thucydides took care to build a single, beautifully-structured argument that was faithful to chronology and took remarkably few liberties with the source materials. He avoided the sort of assumptions that make earlier works frustrating for modern scholars, for example seeking reasons for outcomes that were rooted in human actions and agency, not in the will of the gods. And he was careful to explain where he had obtained much of his information. As a work of structure – and as a work of reasoning – The *History of the Peloponnesian War* continues to inspire, be read and be taught more than 2,000 years after it was written.

ABOUT THE AUTHOR OF THE ORIGINAL WORK

Not much is known about the life of **Thucydides**. He lived in ancient
Greece in the fifth century BCE and was a citizen of Athens. Thucydides
was a general, but he was blamed for the loss of a key city to the enemy,
Sparta, and as a result was sent into exile. This ended his military career, but
opened a new one as a historian.

The *History of the Peloponnesian War* was re-discovered in Western
Europe in the middle ages and first printed in Venice in 1503. Thucydides
has since been hailed as one of the first writers of history as we now know it.

It is uncertain what happened to Thucydides in later life. Some reports
say he was murdered, others say he died while writing his history, others
still that he lived into the fourth century BCE.

ABOUT THE AUTHOR OF THE ANALYSIS

Mark Fisher is a PhD candidate at the University of California, Berkeley
and holds an MPhil in Political Thought and Intellectual History from the
University of Cambridge. His research focuses on Ancient Greek political
thought in the aftermath of the Peloponnesian war.

ABOUT MACAT

GREAT WORKS FOR CRITICAL THINKING

Macat is focused on making the ideas of the world's great thinkers
accessible and comprehensible to everybody, everywhere, in ways that
promote the development of enhanced critical thinking skills.

It works with leading academics from the world's top universities to
produce new analyses that focus on the ideas and the impact of the most
influential works ever written across a wide variety of academic disciplines.
Each of the works that sit at the heart of its growing library is an enduring
example of great thinking. But by setting them in context – and looking
at the influences that shaped their authors, as well as the responses they
provoked – Macat encourages readers to look at these classics and
game-changers with fresh eyes. Readers learn to think, engage and
challenge their ideas, rather than simply accepting them.

'Macat offers an amazing first-of-its-kind tool for interdisciplinary learning and research. Its focus on works that transformed their disciplines and its rigorous approach, drawing on the world's leading experts and educational institutions, opens up a world-class education to anyone.'

Andreas Schleicher
Director for Education and Skills, Organisation for Economic
Co-operation and Development

'Macat is taking on some of the major challenges in university education ... They have drawn together a strong team of active academics who are producing teaching materials that are novel in the breadth of their approach.'

Prof Lord Broers,
former Vice-Chancellor of the University of Cambridge

'The Macat vision is exceptionally exciting. It focuses upon new modes of learning which analyse and explain seminal texts which have profoundly influenced world thinking and so social and economic development. It promotes the kind of critical thinking which is essential for any society and economy. This is the learning of the future.'

Rt Hon Charles Clarke, former UK Secretary of State for Education

'The Macat analyses provide immediate access to the critical conversation surrounding the books that have shaped their respective discipline, which will make them an invaluable resource to all of those, students and teachers, working in the field.'

Professor William Tronzo, University of California at San Diego

WAYS IN TO THE TEXT

KEY POINTS

- Thucydides was a general, and later a writer, from the Greek city-state of Athens. He lived in the fifth century B.C.E. and is credited with practically founding modern, objective, history writing.

- His *History of the Peloponnesian War* is a thorough and balanced account of the first two decades of the war between the two leading Greek city-states of Athens and Sparta. Valued for its attention to accuracy and insightful analysis, the book is taken as a founding document for several schools of thought.

- Thucydides went beyond his careful analysis of the Peloponnesian War* to consider forces in human society that seem just as relevant today.

Who Was Thucydides?

Little is known of the life of the historian Thucydides, author of the *History of the Peloponnesian War*. We know he was a citizen of the Greek city–state of Athens in the fifth century b.c.e., and that he had roots in Thrace* (an ancient region of the Eastern Mediterranean divided by what is today Greece, Turkey, and Bulgaria). He is thought to have been born around 460 b.c.e.; certainly he could not have been born later than 454 b.c.e., since in 424 b.c.e. he was elected one of the 10 generals leading the city-state's efforts in the brutal 27-year-long Peloponnesian War—a post that required a minimum age of 30.

He was banished from Athens soon after his election, however, held responsible for the loss to Sparta of a strategic city. Although exile ended Thucydides' military career, it allowed him to take up a new one as a historian. He went on to write a history of the war: the *History* for which he is famous today. The work breaks off in 411 b.c.e. after recording the first 20 years of the conflict, though parts of the text appear to have been written after Athens's final surrender to Sparta in 404. Lacking any record of Thucydides' death, however, we cannot be sure when he died.

Thucydides is often considered the founder of modern history writing. Unlike those writers of his time who were somewhat less than meticulous with their facts and timelines, Thucydides took factual accuracy to be of the highest importance and based his history on the evidence he could gather. This included both what he saw during his time as a general and conversations with many others who were involved in the war. He denied any role for the gods in his history, seeking instead to analyze the reasons that nations and individuals made the decisions they did. Finally, he wrote a history that was impartial, not favoring any side over the other.

What Does *History of the Peloponnesian War* Say?

Thucydides' *History of the Peloponnesian War* is the main source of information we have on that important and lengthy conflict between the two Greek city-states of Athens and Sparta; the destructive war ended up not only engulfing all of Greece, as other cities lined up behind one side or the other, but eventually, with the entry of Sicily and Persia into the war, most of the Eastern Mediterranean as well.

Not only is the book our main source of information on the war, it is a very good quality source: well researched and carefully assembled, often presenting lengthy opposing arguments to provide readers with an in-depth understanding of the thoughts and justifications of the various participants in the conflict, and a thoughtful and unbiased analysis of events.

Since its rediscovery in the period of European history known as the Renaissance* (a time marking the end of the medieval period, when artists, writers, architects, and musicians turned towards the arts and literature of ancient Rome and Greece to reinvigorate European culture), the book has had a constant place among the leading works of Western intellectual life.

It has had a significant impact on a number of leading Western thinkers, among them the English philosopher Thomas Hobbes,* the Scottish philosopher David Hume,* and the German philosopher Friedrich Nietzsche.*

More recently, Thucydides' work has become a key text for several academic disciplines, notably classical history (that is, the history of ancient Greece and Rome), military history, political science, and international relations (the study of the interactions of nation states). It is in this last academic branch that Thucydides has had a particularly strong influence.

For most of the twentieth century, what is known as "realism"* has been a highly influential school of thought in the field of international relations. According to this approach, relations among countries are anarchic, amoral, and self-interested. It suggests that countries should shape their policies to promote stability and their own security, rather than be guided by considerations of morality.

But while this approach had a large following during the Cold War* (a long period of diplomatic hostility between the Soviet Union and its allies and the United States and its allies that began in the 1940s), it has lost much of its appeal since the collapse of the Soviet Union in 1989. Significantly, however, the scholars who have pushed aside international relations realism have not abandoned Thucydides in the process. Rather, they have argued that viewing the book as supporting realism is the result of a shallow and selective reading of the work.

These anti-realism scholars argue that a more accurate reading of Thucydides shows him to reject realism and support their approach.

Thucydides' work remains an important text, especially in the two disciplines of classics (the study of ancient Greek and Latin literature and philosophy) and political science. In a development welcomed by many scholars, the book, which is hard to pigeonhole into one single academic branch, is promoting the development of interdisciplinary studies (that is, studies that draw on the methods and aims of different academic fields).

In this way, political scientists, historians, and literary scholars are beginning to enter into conversation with one another. Many of the issues Thucydides explored with so much insight more than 2000 years ago seem fresh even today: the reasons countries go to war, the ways democracies can fail to promote the common good both at home and abroad where they control an empire, and the relationship between morality, security, and good leadership in a democracy.

Why Does *History of the Peloponnesian War* Matter?

Thucydides' work was innovative, in that he let his history be guided by a careful and thorough analysis of all the facts and evidence he could gather. In this way he avoided non-scientific factors in his account such as rumors, prejudice, and the supernatural (generally by giving the gods responsibility for events). Although Thucydides lived in a very different time and place, his clear-eyed, evidence-based approach is an inspiration for scholars and students in a variety of disciplines, no less today than it was centuries ago.

The momentous events Thucydides recounts took place almost 2500 years ago. But many of his concerns will be familiar to scholars and students today. He lived at a time of cultural and intellectual upheaval pitting traditionalists who maintained faith in their traditional gods against the more modern-thinking rationalists. In that turmoil, Thucydides strove to fashion his own approach. His aim was to write an accurate and trustworthy account of events that would be accepted as balanced and impartial.

He found the lack of concern for accuracy of facts and timelines that he saw in many writers and in the public at large particularly alarming: "People accept quite uncritically any reports of the past they get from others, even those relating to their own country," he wrote.[1]

Readers today can also find inspiration in the way Thucydides goes from his thorough analyses of why the Peloponnesian War occurred to considering the nearly timeless question of why wars in general take place. Likewise, his close examination of the forces that fueled that ancient conflict leads him to consider, in ways that seem fully relevant today, the impact of self-interest, justice, honor, fortune, hope, fear, and lust.

NOTES

1   Thucydides, *The War of the Peloponnesians and the Athenians*, ed. and trans. Jeremy Mynott (Cambridge: Cambridge University Press, 2013), 14 [1.20.1].

SECTION 1
INFLUENCES

MODULE 1
THE AUTHOR AND THE
HISTORICAL CONTEXT

KEY POINTS

- Thucydides is often considered to have invented the discipline of history, with his clear-eyed, fact-based accounts. He was one of the first writers to analyze events not as caused by the gods, but as the result of the political actions of humans.

- Thucydides was first a young Athenian general in the Peloponnesian War* (a 27-year conflict between Athens, Sparta, and their respective allies in the fifth century B.C.E.), but Athens blamed him for losing a key battle and exiled him. Exile gave him the opportunity to study the war and write about it from a neutral stance.

- The Peloponnesian War dragged almost all of Greece and eventually most of the Eastern Mediterranean into a destructive conflict. But it also gave rise to intense intellectual and artistic creation.

Why Read This Text?

It is difficult to summarize the importance of Thucydides' *History of the Peloponnesian War* for the Western tradition of thinking about history and politics. It is, in the first instance, the primary historical source that we have for events of the Peloponnesian War. More than this, however, it is thought by many to have inaugurated the discipline of history as we know it.

Though the Greek historian Herodotus* had previously written a work on the Persian Wars* that is often called *The Histories*, Thucydides

> ❝ Thucydides of Athens wrote the war of the
> Peloponnesians and the Athenians, how they waged it
> against each other. He began writing at its very outset,
> in the expectation that this would be a great war and
> more worthy of account than any previous one ...
> This was certainly the greatest ever upheaval among
> the Greeks, and one which affected a good part of the
> barbarian world too—even, you could say, most of
> mankind. ❞
>
> Thucydides, *History of the Peloponnesian War*

is the first to use a strict chronological framework for his history, to
ignore the gods as forces that cause events in the human world, and to
hold the accuracy of facts to be of the utmost importance for the
historian as he writes. All of this was a sharp reinvention of how to
understand history and politics (that is, as collective human activity
rather than the actions of gods and other divine forces) and how
individuals might go about understanding and recording it (that is, by
carefully and realistically looking at the observable facts).

Because Thucydides does not just document facts, however, but
also analyzes them and has his characters speculate about them, his
text has proved of lasting interest to those interested in understanding
politics. Thucydides is frequently thought to have inaugurated the
tradition of international relations realism* (an approach to international relations that assumes that nations act out of self-interest, and
that security takes precedence over morality) and his text continues to
provide its readers with careful and clear-eyed insights into the tense
relationships between power, morality, and security in political life.

His text has had an important impact on a number of the West's
most significant modern political thinkers, notably the English
philosopher Thomas Hobbes,* the Scottish philosopher David

Hume,* and the German philosopher Friedrich Nietzsche,* to name a few. Thucydides has influenced more recent politics, too; while serving as the chairman of the joint chiefs of staff, for instance, the American military leader Colin Powell* hung a quote from Thucydides in his office, and Irving Kristol,* the so-called godfather of the aggressive, right-wing political movement known as neoconservatism,* once claimed, "The favorite neoconservative text on foreign affairs ... is Thucydides on the Peloponnesian War."[1]

Author's Life

Not much is known about Thucydides beyond what he says about himself in this text, which is little. From what we can piece together, Thucydides was an Athenian (a citizen of the Greek city-state of Athens), who had roots and influence in the Eastern Mediterranean region of Thrace,* a nation on the borders of what is today Bulgaria, Turkey, and Greece. He was likely a relative of the Athenian statesman Cimon* and therefore part of a leading Athenian family.[2] He was elected one of the 10 Athenian generals in 424 B.C.E., making him at least 30 years old at this time and a capable politician. Soon after this, however, he was exiled from Athens for the remainder of the war following the loss of the city of Amphipolis,* for which he was held responsible.[3] It is unclear where or how he spent these years, but some doubtful stories of ancient origin survive about him.[4]

Though we know so little about Thucydides, we can see that he was in a unique position to write the work that he did. For a time, he was an active participant in the Peloponnesian War and an Athenian who had reached the highest levels of power, giving him a deep insight into the war. But then he fell out of favor. With a vote of the Athenian assembly—the gathering of citizens with final decision-making power in the city-state—he was exiled from Athens and removed from the war effort.

Although this must have been devastating for Thucydides at the time, eventually he came to appreciate that exile brought with it certain advantages. "It so turned out," he wrote, "that I was banished from my own country for twenty years after the Amphipolis campaign and thus had the time to study matters more closely; and as a consequence of my exile I had access to activities on both sides, not least to those of the Peloponnesians."[5] In ending his military career, exile promoted Thucydides' literary career. It also enabled him to adopt an impartial approach in his writing, favoring neither side.

Author's Background

The Peloponnesian War (431–404 B.C.E.) was a long and often brutal conflict fought between the Spartans (citizens of the Greek city-state of Sparta) and the Athenians. Thucydides judged that this was the most important conflict that the world had ever seen, and as such it was "most worthy of being talked about." In part this was because each of these cities was extremely powerful in their own right. But it was also because of the large number of dependent "allies" that each commanded. Between the two of them, these alliances involved nearly the whole of Greece in the war, on one side or the other. When the Sicilians and the Persians eventually entered into the war as well, the conflict enveloped most of the Eastern Mediterranean, becoming for the Greeks something of a "world war" (as Thucydides describes it, it included "the greater part of mankind").[6]

Thucydides was not the only Athenian, nor the only Greek, who had his life defined and turned upside down by the war. The war was an ever-present and often devastating part of Greek life in the late fifth century B.C.E. This was particularly true in Athens, where the onset of plague and the siege-like conditions in which the people lived for much of the time caused great suffering and disrupted traditional ways of life. Thucydides himself suffered from the plague and survived, and he offers a rich portrait of both the disease and its effects on social life in Athens.[7]

Despite the intense suffering associated with these years (or perhaps because of it), the final third of the fifth century was also a period of philosophical innovation and artistic achievement. These were the years when the enormously influential philosopher Socrates* roamed the streets of Athens, and traveling teachers and scholars known as sophists,* of whom the most famous are perhaps Protagoras*and Gorgias,* traveled from across Greece to lecture in the city. These years also saw the production of such iconic plays as *Oedipus the King* by the playwright Sophocles,* and *Medea* and *Bacchae* by Euripides,* not to mention most of the works by the playwright Aristophanes.* It appears it was as rich an intellectual environment as the world has ever seen, and it shaped Thucydides' development as a thinker.

NOTES

1   Shifra Sharlin, "Thucydides and the Powell Doctrine," *Raritan* 24, no. 1 (2004): 12–28; Irving Kristol, "The Neoconservative Persuasion," *The Weekly Standard*, August 25, 2003, accessed April 22, 2015, http://www.weeklystandard.com/Content/Public/Articles/000/000/003/000tzmlw.asp.

2   For Thucydides' influence in Thrace, see his own comments in *History of the Peloponnesian War* 4.105.1.

3   See Thucydides' account of this in *History of the Peloponnesian War* 4.102–7. On his exile, see also 5.26.5.

4   These accounts are often of doubtful historical truth, however, and they probably give us a better sense of what other Greeks thought about Thucydides than the actual facts of the author's life. For discussions of problems in the biography of Thucydides, see L. Canfora, "Biographical Obscurities and Problems of Composition," in *Brill's Companion to Thucydides*, ed. Antonios Rengakos and Antonis Tsakmakis (Leiden: Brill, 2006), 3–32; and Judith Maitland, "Marcellinus' Life of Thucydides: Criticism and Criteria in the Ancient Biographical Tradition," *Classical Quarterly* 46, no. 2 (1996): 538–58.

5   *History of the Peloponnesian War* 5.26.5.

6   *History of the Peloponnesian War* 1.1.1.

7   *History of the Peloponnesian War* 2.47–54.

MODULE 2
ACADEMIC CONTEXT

KEY POINTS

- Intellectually, Thucydides came of age in an Athens torn between traditional and new visions of man's place in the world.

- Thucydides was influenced by the sophists*—traveling scholars and teachers who proposed rational thinking and rejected the traditional Greek view that mankind was subject to the whim of the gods.

- Thucydides' text bears the marks of both sides in the argument, straddling the gap between radical thinkers and traditional ideas.

The Work in its Context

By all accounts, Thucydides was an original thinker. His originality grew out of his readiness to borrow from the rich and varied intellectual environment in which he lived and his eagerness to stand against it in his *History of the Peloponnesian War*.

The intellectual world in which Thucydides came of age as a thinker was, in many ways, at odds with itself. Greece as a whole was full of political and cultural divisions, and Athens in particular saw an intense period of cultural turmoil and change. In particular, the years of the Peloponnesian War* saw a clash between those who wanted to uphold the traditional customs and values of Athens and those who wanted to rethink Athenian political life with radically new ideas based on rationalism and self-interest.

At the forefront of those who offered new ideas about the human condition were the sophists, a group of traveling intellectuals and

> **❝** From the evidence I have presented ... one would not go wrong in supposing that events were much as I have set them out; and no one should prefer rather to believe the songs of the poets, who exaggerate things for artistic purposes, or the writings of the chroniclers, which are composed more to make good listening than to represent the truth. **❞**
>
> Thucydides, *History of the Peloponnesian War*

teachers who had a significant impact on the thinkers of Athens. The sophists were never strongly linked with one another, and they often disagreed among themselves. Yet they are thought to have shared a similarly skeptical outlook and egoism—seeing self-interest as the root of morality. This skepticism posed a challenge to the traditional Athenian values, and especially to the traditional belief in the gods. In a break with those beliefs, the sophists saw the basis of ethics—the search for a moral code—in the pursuit of an individual's or group's interests.

Throughout the Peloponnesian War, however, there were many who remained loyal to the older Athenian traditions, and who were themselves skeptical of the sophists' teachings. Rather than turning to the sophists for their education, they continued to turn towards the poets Homer* and Hesiod,* and other respected poets of previous generations, and maintained the traditional beliefs and practices of Athenian civic religion.[1]

Overview of the Field

Both the advocates for tradition and those for change were loose groups, and neither had a program laid out in a key text. One work, however, looms largest in Greek culture of the fifth century: Homer's

Iliad. The *Iliad* is the epic poem of the anger of the Greek warrior Achilles, set against the backdrop of the legendary Trojan War,* fought between the Greeks and the people of the city of Troy. It is a story about conflict, and it depicts a world in which the gods frequently and coldly set men against one another for their own ends. In this story, it is the gods, in the end, who determine human action, and their meddling results in both glory and suffering for the humans involved.

For the supporters of tradition, the *Iliad* and other poetic works contained all there was to know about the human condition and how to live one's life honorably. The authority of these works, however, relied largely on the poets' claims to divine inspiration—the gods inspired their poetry. But sophists, like Protagoras,* attacked such claims.

Protagoras was skeptical of the "unseen" knowledge that poets, priests, and other traditional authority figures were supposed to have access to.[2] He instead encouraged a type of inquiry that was limited to what ordinary human beings could observe. This, it seems, is what he meant when he said that "Man is the measure of all things—of the things that are, that they are, and of the things that are not, that they are not."[3] Such a view did not have room for the invisible role of the gods, and Protagoras was dismissive of belief that the gods caused events to happen on earth.

Academic Influences

Thucydides would eventually try to bridge the gap between Homer and Protagoras—but he was not the first to do so. A generation before Thucydides, the historian Herodotus* wrote an "inquiry" (*historiê*) into the Persian Wars* that made such an attempt.[4] In length, structure, and subject, Herodotus's work was epic, documenting as it did the rise of the Persians from humble beginnings to greatness, and their crashing defeat at the hands of the Greeks. However, in its intellectual approach and style, Herodotus's text shows the strong influence of the sophists and the Hippocratics,* a movement devoted to the study of disease as a natural phenomenon, not something caused by gods or evil spells. This is apparent in Herodotus's choice of the word *historiê* for his work, as this was a buzzword for inquiry in the sophistic style. Similarly, Herodotus identifies himself, and not divine inspiration, as the source of his *historiê*.[5]

Thucydides' relationship with Herodotus, as with Homer, Protagoras, and the Hippocratic medical tradition, is not easy to define.[6] Thucydides sets himself clearly at odds with the Greek tradition in his work, complaining that both poets and writers distorted the facts in their accounts. After his own version of the Trojan and Persian Wars, Thucydides states, "From the evidence I have presented … one would not go wrong in supposing that events were much as I have set them out; and no one should prefer rather to believe the songs of the poets, who exaggerate things for artistic purposes, or the writings of the chroniclers, which are composed more to make good listening than to represent the truth."[7]

But this is not the whole story. Despite Thucydides' open opposition to them, he is deeply indebted to both the Homeric and the sophistic traditions, and especially to Herodotus's earlier attempt to merge the two.[8] More than a first attempt to write modern history, it can be helpful to read Thucydides' *History* as a second attempt, after Herodotus, to create a new type of Homeric epic using the rationalism of the sophists.

NOTES

1   This is a very general account of a complex historical period. For much more nuanced accounts, see G. E. R. Lloyd, *The Revolutions in Wisdom: Studies in the Claims and Practice of Ancient Greek Science* (Berkeley, CA: University of California Press, 1987); Leslie Kurke, *Coins, Bodies, Games, and Gold: The Politics of Meaning in Archaic Greece* (Princeton, NJ: Princeton University Press, 1999). More specifically on the sophists, see W. K. C. Guthrie, *The Sophists* (Cambridge: Cambridge University Press, 1971); and G. B. Kerferd, *The Sophistic Movement* (Cambridge: Cambridge University Press, 1981).

2   It can be very difficult to reconstruct Protagoras's thought, as there is little direct evidence of his teachings that remain. Much of what we do think we know comes from Plato, but it has long been doubted whether he is a faithful witness. See, for instance, Cynthia Farrar, *The Origins of Democratic Thinking: The Invention of Politics in Classical Athens* (Cambridge: Cambridge University Press, 1988).

3   Robin Waterfield, trans., *The First Philosophers: The Presocratics and the Sophists* (Oxford: Oxford University Press, 2000), 211.

4   Herodotus, *Histories* 1.1.1.

5   See Rosalind Thomas, *Herodotus in Context: Ethnography, Science and the Art of Persuasion* (Cambridge: Cambridge University Press, 2002). See also Leslie Kurke, "Charting the Poles of History: Herodotus and Thoukydides," in *Literature in the Greek and Roman Worlds: A New Perspective*, ed. Oliver Taplin (Oxford: Oxford University Press, 2000), 133–55.

6   The complexity of Thucydides' relationship to the Hippocratic medical tradition has been the subject of a number of good recent studies. See Rosalind Thomas, "Thucydides' Intellectual Milieu and the Plague," in *Brill's Companion to Thucydides*, ed. Antonios Rengakos and Antonis Tsakmakis (Leiden: Brill, 2006), 87–108; and Jacques Jouanna, "Cause and Crisis in Historians and Medical Writers of the Classical Period," in *Hippocrates in Context: Papers Read at the 11th International Hippocrates Colloquium, University of Newcastle upon Tyne, August 27–31, 2002*, ed. Philip van der Eijk (Leiden: Brill, 2005).

7   Thucydides, *The War of the Peloponnesians and the Athenians*, ed. and trans. Jeremy Mynott (Cambridge: Cambridge University Press, 2013), 14 [1.21.1].

8   For a recent collection of essays that explore this theme, see Edith Foster and Donald Lateiner, eds., *Thucydides and Herodotus* (Oxford: Oxford University Press, 2012).

MODULE 3
THE PROBLEM

KEY POINTS

- Thucydides' central concern was to provide an accurate and unbiased understanding of what happened in the Peloponnesian War,* and why.

- There appears to have been an intense debate at the time about the events of the Peloponnesian War. Thucydides sought to provide an authoritative version, and beyond that, he looked at why wars in general happen.

- Thucydides' book has much in common with accounts of wars by the poet Homer* and the historian Herodotus.* Yet he criticizes them for a lack of concern over the accuracy of what they report.

Core Question

Though Thucydides' book is now read as one of the key works of Western political theory, the questions he strove to answer in the *History of the Peloponnesian War* were practical. Thucydides wanted to know exactly what happened in the Peloponnesian War and its run-up, and why it happened.

Though evidence here is slim, we can imagine that Thucydides was hardly alone in pursuing such questions. The war would have been of life and death importance for most Greeks during this period. There would have been an enormous need for reliable information, both to plan for the future and to hold various groups and individuals accountable for their behavior. After the war, moreover, we can expect the Athenians to have given much thought to the events and causes that led to their defeat, loss of empire, and descent into civil war.[1]

> **❝** [This work] will have served its purpose well enough if it is judged useful by those who want to have a clear view of what happened in the past and what—the human condition being what it is—can be expected to happen again some time in the future in similar or much the same ways. It is composed to be a possession for all time and not just a performance-piece for the moment. **❞**
>
> Thucydides, *History of the Peloponnesian War*

In addressing the questions that would have been on everyone's mind, Thucydides insisted on answering them according to his own intellectual orientation. In particular, Thucydides was sharply critical of what he took to be the popular disregard for accuracy in answering such questions; as he writes, "People accept quite uncritically any reports of the past they get from others, even those relating to their own country."[2] He found the Athenians to be no different, and he criticizes them for romanticizing and thereby misunderstanding their own history.

In offering his own account of what happened in the Peloponnesian War and why it happened, Thucydides sets himself on a different path. In relating the events (the word he uses is *erga*) of the war, he writes, "I resolved not to rely in my writing on what I learned from chance sources or even on my own impressions, but both in the cases where I was present myself and in those where I depended on others I investigated every detail with the utmost concern for accuracy. This was a laborious process of research, because eyewitnesses at the various events reported the same things differently, depending on which side they favored and on their powers of memory."[3]

The Participants

Against these different eyewitness accounts, Thucydides wanted his own account of the Peloponnesian War to be trustworthy and authoritative. It can be easy to forget that in the apparently unexciting retelling of each event—that so many men sailed from this port to that, for example—Thucydides is likely weighing in on a pointed debate among his contemporaries over what happened at this point. This is easy to overlook, in part, because Thucydides kept such debates out of his text, simply stating the truth as he judged it to be.

But it is also easy to overlook because we simply lack sufficient evidence from the time to establish who the participants in these debates were and what they were arguing. We can imagine that they were many, and that their disagreements were heated, but unfortunately Thucydides stands as the only source that we have for many of the events he describes.

Nevertheless, from the works that do remain to us, we are able to appreciate that Thucydides was participating in a long-standing conversation about how to understand great wars, not just the local debates about what happened in the Peloponnesian War. In this, Thucydides was in direct conversation with both Herodotus, author of *The Histories*, and Homer, author of the *Iliad*, and the question of why did *this* war happen merges into the question of why do wars *in general* happen.

In the epics of Homer, it is the gods who cause wars. In the first lines of the *Iliad*, for instance, Zeus is credited with directing the action of the entire story.[4] Herodotus's analysis is more subtle, and, in the style of the traveling teachers of philosophy called the sophists,* more rational. Although he does not deny that the gods play some significant part, he is doubtful of the Greek myths about them, and he is often more interested in the immediate, down-to-earth causes that push men to war.

The Contemporary Debate

Thucydides' relationship to Homer and Herodotus was complicated, much like his relationship with Protagoras* and the sophists. To an extent, Thucydides was a severe critic of all their works. He believed that Homer's and Herodotus's accounts of great war suffered from the same weaknesses as the people's beliefs—they did not value accuracy.[5] And yet, it is important to see that he still follows their lead in choosing his subject and constructing his story. Not only are all three works dramatic accounts of war that are longer and more complete than other histories, but each offers a balanced account of the two sides to these wars, refusing to tell the story from just one side.

Moreover, many scholars have noticed many direct allusions to Herodotus's *Histories* and Homer's *Iliad* in Thucydides' text.[6] Perhaps most striking are the similarities between Thucydides' account of the decision of Athens to attack Sicily* and Herodotus's account of the Persian king Xerxes'* decision to attack Greece.[7] But even in such places, Thucydides' account does not simply mirror that of the earlier writers. He is constantly remaking the patterns and explanations from the other books that he is hinting at, reworking them to account for his own strict concern for accuracy and the actual events of the war.

Thucydides encourages the reader to understand his work as having timeless importance. He says that he has written the work as a "possession for all time" (*ktêma es aieî*).[8] Thucydides has come stunningly close to realizing his ambition, and yet it is important for the reader to remember that he was a fifth-century B.C.E. Athenian. In the creation of what he hoped would be seen as eternal wisdom, Thucydides borrowed heavily from a number of different cultural traditions of his day and was in conversation with the great works of Greek literature. Without some understanding of these traditions, and especially of works like the *Iliad* and Herodotus's *Histories*, it can be very easy to miss this, leaving one with the impression that Thucydides was the isolated figure that he portrays himself to be.

NOTES

1   This is suggested by Xenophon's account of the Athenians' mindset as defeat was imminent. See Xenophon, *Hellenica* 2.2.3, 2.2.10.

2   Thucydides, *The War of the Peloponnesians and the Athenians*, ed. and trans. Jeremy Mynott (Cambridge: Cambridge University Press, 2013), 14 [1.20.1].

3   Thucydides, *The War of the Peloponnesians and the Athenians*, 15 [1.22.2].

4   Homer, *Iliad*, line 5.

5   Thucydides, *The War of the Peloponnesians and the Athenians*, 14 [1.21.1].

6   For a recent collection of essays that explore this theme, see Edith Foster and Donald Lateiner, eds., *Thucydides and Herodotus* (Oxford: Oxford University Press, 2012).

7   See, for instance, Richard Ned Lebow, *The Tragic Vision of Politics: Ethics, Interests and Orders* (Cambridge: Cambridge University Press, 2003), 135. This parallel is also developed by many essays in Foster and Lateiner, eds., *Thucydides and Herodotus*.

8   Thucydides, *The War of the Peloponnesians and the Athenians*, 15–16 [1.22.4].

MODULE 4
THE AUTHOR'S CONTRIBUTION

KEY POINTS

- Thucydides admits that the speeches of key figures that he reproduces in his work may not be as accurate as the rest of the book.

- While previous great writers were fuzzy about the time periods and order in which events they described took place, Thucydides' quest for accuracy led him to place events in a clear chronological framework.

- Thucydides noted with dismay how the decency and nobility of life in Athens fell apart during the war.

Author's Aims

Thucydides' chief concern in *History of the Peloponnesian War* was accuracy; his main complaint against the great writers who came before him was that they distorted the accounts they told. But it was no simple task for Thucydides to write more accurately than those he criticized. He accepted that his concern for the truth would have to have certain limitations, and it would greatly limit what he was able to write about.

In terms of limitations, Thucydides states to his readers outright that the speeches of the key figures that he included in his *History* do not maintain the same strict loyalty to what happened as the rest of the book's narrative. Speeches were harder to remember than events, Thucydides says, and as a result he aimed for a sort of compromise between presenting an accurate account in the speeches and writing what he believed the speakers should have said. Thucydides explained, "What I have set down is how I think each of them would have

> ❝ So it was that every kind of wickedness took root in Greece as a result of these civil conflicts. Simplicity of spirit, which is such an important part of true nobility, was laughed to scorn and vanished, while people were largely divided into opposite and mutually suspicious camps. ❞
>
> Thucydides, *History of the Peloponnesian War*

expressed what was most appropriate in the particular circumstances, while staying as close as possible to the overall intention of what was actually said."[1]

Because Thucydides was looking for accuracy in the realm of humanly observable facts, he was led to write only about human and other natural forces acting in the historical process, thus eliminating supernatural forces entirely from his account. This does not mean that the gods are left out entirely from Thucydides' work. Thucydides talks about the extent to which widespread belief in the gods frequently impacted the course of the Peloponnesian War.* But it was the human belief that Thucydides was interested in, and that he thought was a force of history, not the gods themselves.

Approach

Accuracy demanded two further things of Thucydides' approach. The first was a chronological framework for his narrative. Unlike Herodotus,* who moved back and forth through time fluidly and was often woolly on questions of chronological order, Thucydides reports the events of the Peloponnesian War precisely according to years and seasons. In so doing, it has been argued, he took an important step away from the more free-floating, mythological conception of time, and towards the invention of historical time as we now know it.[2]

Thucydides was trying to do more than just this, however. In tying each event to a particular historical moment, he was also attempting to introduce a standardized framework for all of Greece to replace the various local ways in which cities kept track of the years (in Athens, for example, each year was named after the official who held the senior governmental post of eponymous archon* as chief magistrate for a year).

Thucydides' insistence on tying the events he writes about to a chronological framework—clearly indicating the order in which events took place, with at least approximate dates—was decisive in the early development of the Western approach to history writing. In fact, it is difficult for us today to imagine "history" that does not frame its accounts in this way.

The second demand that accuracy made on Thucydides' approach is more counterintuitive in that it seems to go against our present ideas of what history is. Thucydides did not believe that much could be said accurately about the past. Too much was unknown and disputed, and the best one could often do was to establish what was likely to have happened. The present, however, was different, and Thucydides believed that it alone could be written about accurately.

In this way, Thucydides was different from the historians of our day, and from Herodotus and Homer.* Herodotus wrote about a war that was half a century old, and Homer, whether he was an actual man or a tradition of poets, composed a poem about the mythological past that was not set at any particular time. In a subtle barb aimed at these two writers, Thucydides describes all that he thought could be reliably known about the Trojan War* (the legendary conflict that Homer described) and the Persian Wars* (the actual conflict that Herodotus wrote about) in about 10 pages.[3] Moreover, of what he writes, much is framed in the language of probability ("It was likely the case that ..."). To write accurately and in detail about a war, Thucydides insisted, one had to live through it.

Contribution in Context

Thucydides' concern for accuracy set him apart from Homer and Herodotus, but it set him into a more complicated relationship with the rational, intellectual sophists* such as Protagoras* and related movements such as the Hippocratic* medical writers.

Thucydides agreed with them that it was natural forces—people or nature—and not the gods that caused historical events. He also resembles the sophists in his frequent presentation of paired speeches from two figures with opposing positions, his interest in political rhetoric (that is, the theory and practice of persuasive language), and his belief that humans are often motivated by a self-interest and the quest for prestige or power.

Unlike sophists such as Protagoras, however, who often found their teachings socially liberating, Thucydides viewed the erosion of the old way of life in Greece with considerable reluctance. "Simplicity of spirit, which is such an important part of true nobility, was laughed to scorn and vanished," he wrote of the time during the civil war that eventually engulfed most Greek cities.[4]

Likewise, Thucydides seemed to accept only with a tragic sense of regret that individuals were ceaselessly self-aggrandizing—trying to make themselves seem important.[5] As he also wrote about civil war, for instance, "At the root of all this was the desire for power, based on personal greed and ambition, and the consequent fanaticism of those competing for control."[6] Rather than identifying self-interest as a progressive and positive force, Thucydides shows considerable pessimism about the consequences of humanity's self-assertiveness.

NOTES

1   Thucydides, *The War of the Peloponnesians and the Athenians*, ed. and trans. Jeremy Mynott (Cambridge: Cambridge University Press, 2013), 15 [1.22.1].

2   See Bernard Williams, *Truth and Truthfulness* (Princeton, NJ: Princeton University Press, 2002), 149–71.

3   *History of the Peloponnesian War* 1.2–19.

4   *History of the Peloponnesian War* 3.83.1, 2214.

5   See, for instance, Jacqueline de Romilly, *The Rise and Fall of States According to Greek Authors* (Ann Arbor, MI: University of Michigan Press, 1977), 46–61.

6   Thucydides, *The War of the Peloponnesians and the Athenians*, 213 [3.82.8].

SECTION 2
IDEAS

MODULE 5
MAIN IDEAS

KEY POINTS

- Central themes of Thucydides' political thought emerge from the *History of the Peloponnesian War*, including the relationship between reality and people's self-interested descriptions of reality, and the forces determining political judgment such as justice and advantage.

- Thucydides' views are often unclear. Scholars are at odds as to how to interpret his evaluation of Pericles* and the cause of the Peloponnesian War.*

- Thucydides' language is often very difficult, resulting in a text that appears to support many different readings.

Key Themes

Thucydides' *History of the Peloponnesian War* is mostly a story with particular events presented in chronological order. But at the same time, the book is in some ways a general analysis of war. The *History* includes frequent interruptions of the narrative to present speeches by key figures in the story, as well as Thucydides' own analyses. At these points, a number of themes emerge as central to Thucydides' political thought.

One such theme is the difficult relationship between reality (*ergon*) and how people think and speak about reality (*logos*). This theme frames Thucydides' concern for accuracy, especially in the face of what he sees as an unfortunate lack of concern for accuracy among the Athenian public and the poet Homer* and the historian Herodotus.* The most famous instance of this is the picture he paints of Athens under the leadership of the famous statesman Pericles. He writes that

> 66 As long as [Pericles] was the city's leader in the time of peace he ruled them with moderation and kept Athens safe and secure, and under him it reached the height of its greatness, and after the war broke out he then too showed himself a far-sighted judge of the city's strengths. 99
>
> Thucydides, *History of the Peloponnesian War*

the city was run "in name a democracy [but] in practice government by the foremost man."[1] More subtly, this theme emerges through Thucydides' juxtaposition of speeches and his narratives of the events that follow. At these points, the reader is encouraged to think back on the speakers and evaluate their predictions, judging how they did or did not understand what was about to happen.[2]

Another theme is political motivation and political judgment. Thucydides is interested in the natural forces (as opposed to the gods) that cause political figures to behave the way they do, for better and for worse. These forces include self-interest, justice, honor, fortune, hope, fear, and lust. In this vein, Thucydides' text is most famous for its penetrating picture of the relationship between self-interest and justice. This occurs most strikingly in the Melian dialogue,* his account of the Athenians' attempts to persuade the Melian people to join their empire. In this part of the text, the Athenians defend their aggressive and imperialist policy by stating that justice is not an issue between the strong and the weak. Rather, "the possibilities are defined by what the strong do and the weak accept."[3]

Exploring the Ideas

Although it is easy to see the central themes in Thucydides' text, there is widespread disagreement over what Thucydides is trying to argue. Two points of disagreement that have been particularly central are

Thucydides' identification of the cause of the war, and what he thinks imperial Athens's view of itself and its policies was at the peak of its power.

Thucydides states his view of the war's cause with clarity: "I consider the truest cause, though the one least openly stated, to be this: the Athenians were becoming powerful and inspired fear in the Spartans and so were forced into war."[4]

Despite its directness, there is a lack of clarity in what Thucydides is claiming. Grammatically, it is unclear who it is forcing whom into war. Scholars have suggested both Athens and Sparta, but perhaps the most convincing reading of the sentence is that of the classical scholar Martin Ostwald,* who argues that Athens and Sparta, together, forced one another into war.[5] Beyond this grammatical fuzziness, scholars have also disagreed over Thucydides' belief in this claim. It has been argued, for instance, that Thucydides did not think that war was "necessary" in any real sense, but rather that it occurred because of the widespread belief in its necessity.[6]

Scholars have also disagreed over Thucydides' opinion of Athens's leader Pericles, his war strategy, and his vision of imperial, democratic Athens. Again, Thucydides offers what looks like a clear indication of his thoughts on this matter. Thucydides claims that as long as Pericles was the leader of Athens during peacetime, "he ruled them with moderation and kept Athens safe and secure, and under him it reached the height of its greatness; and after the war broke out he then showed himself a far-sighted judge of the city's strengths."[7]

This is strong praise from Thucydides, and it continues as he suggests that the death of Pericles was the key moment in Athens's defeat. After Pericles died, he states, the Athenians took a selfish turn, giving up on Pericles' far-sighted war policy for one that was riskier but better satisfied private ambitions. Ultimately, this policy caused Athens's defeat by encouraging poor judgment on the part of leaders and people and by leading to civil war in the city, which Thucydides identifies as the immediate cause of the defeat of Athens.

As with Thucydides' identification of the war's cause, scholars have disagreed over how we should read this passage. While some want to take it as a clear sign that Thucydides was a supporter of Pericles, writing perhaps to defend his honor after Athens's defeat, others suggest that is an ironic rhetorical ploy, encouraging the reader to identify with a view that will later be shown as false.[8]

Language and Expression

It can be hard to understand how Thucydides' text could lead to so many contrary interpretations. Some of the disagreement over Thucydides' ideas, however, stems from the difficulty of Thucydides' writing style and the subtlety of his dramatic technique. Thucydides' Greek is often very dense, counterintuitive, and puzzling. When we add to this the extremely complex way in which he constructs his narratives, and especially the way in which he places certain speeches of key figures opposite relevant text passages, as well as speech opposite speech, it leaves the reader with a wide range of ideas to take in.

Thucydides leaves it up to the reader to make clear the meaning of it all. He or she must interpret what the German philosopher Friedrich Nietzsche* called Thucydides' "unuttered thoughts."[9] The French classicist Jacqueline de Romilly* has called it Thucydides' "art of implied meaning."[10] By leaving so much unsaid, Thucydides created a text of great literary artistry—although scholars understand various passages, if not the whole work, in different ways.

It is interesting to note that Thucydides' ancient biographer, Marcellinus, detected a clearly elitist element to Thucydides' puzzling style. He wrote that Thucydides was "deliberately obscure, not wishing to be accessible to everyone or to cheapen his reputation by being easily understood by any casual reader; rather, he wanted the esteem and admiration of the real intelligentsia."[11]

NOTES

1   Thucydides, *The War of the Peloponnesians and the Athenians*, ed. and trans. Jeremy Mynott (Cambridge: Cambridge University Press, 2013), 130 [2.65.9].

2   The now classic study on speech and action in Thucydides is Adam Parry, Logos *and* Ergon *in Thucydides* (New York: Arno Press, 1981).

3   Thucydides, *The War of the Peloponnesians and the Athenians*, 380 [5.84–114, quote at 5.89].

4   Thucydides, *The War of the Peloponnesians and the Athenians* (slightly amended), 16 [1.23.6].

5   Martin Ostwald, *in Thucydides* (Atlanta, GA: Scholars Press, 1988), 1–4.

6   See Hans-Peter Stahl, *Thucydides: Man's Place in History* (Swansea: Classical Press of Wales, 2003 [1966]), 37–61; Geoffrey Hawthorne, *Thucydides and Politics: Back to the Present* (Cambridge: Cambridge University Press, 2014), 39–50.

7   Thucydides, *The War of the Peloponnesians and the Athenians*, 129 [2.65.5].

8   For these contrasting views, see Donald Kagan, *Thucydides: The Reinvention of History* (New York: Viking Press, 2009), 75; and W. R. Connor, *Thucydides* (Princeton, NJ: Princeton University Press, 1984), 59–63, 73–75.

9   Friedrich Nietzsche, "Twilight of the Idols," in *Twilight of the Idols with The Antichrist and Ecce Homo*, trans. A. Ludovici (Ware: Wordsworth Editions, 2007), 85.

10 Jacqueline de Romilly, *The Mind of Thucydides*, trans. E. Rawlings (Ithaca, NY: Cornell University Press, 2012 [1967]), 49–59. The German philosopher Friedrich Nietzsche called these Thucydides' "unuttered thoughts," and he wrote, "there are few thinkers so rich in unuttered thoughts." Nietzsche, "Twilight of the Idols," 85.

11 In Thucydides, *The War of the Peloponnesians and the Athenians*, 604.

MODULE 6
SECONDARY IDEAS

KEY POINTS

- The *History of the Peloponnesian War* presents and discusses many factors that explain why Athens descended into a destructive civil war and eventually lost the war with Sparta.

- Thucydides explores the competing ideas of what it means to act in one's self-interest. He considers in depth Athens's decision to conquer the neutral Melian people, but, to the frustration of many, he does not say which side he thought was right.

- Research in Thucydides' *History* poses difficulties for today's scholars, who are often limited by the divisions between modern academic disciplines.

Other Ideas

Thucydides' *History of the Peloponnesian War* is incredibly rich in ideas, especially in speeches of key participants in the events and analytic passages, even if these do not all point in the same direction. Even in his most direct account of why Athens ultimately lost the war, Thucydides pieces together what we might consider to be a number of different causes: the death of the Athenian leader Pericles,* the change in Athens's political motivation, policy disasters such as the one in Sicily, and civil war.

Thucydides saw a range of other forces at work in political life too; facts such as hope, national character, and plague, to say nothing of the political forms of democracy, aristocracy, and tyranny, also receive significant attention. Thucydides sees political life as the place where

> ❝ In the case of the gods we believe, and in the case
> of humankind it has always been obvious, that as a
> necessity of nature wherever anyone has the upper
> hand they rule. We were not the ones to lay down this
> law, nor the first to take advantage of its existence. We
> found it already established, expect to leave it to last for
> ever, and now make use of it, knowing full well that you
> and anyone else who enjoyed the same power as we do
> would act in just the same way. ❞
>
> Thucydides, *History of the Peloponnesian War*

all these forces, as well as others, interact. He thought it important to account for each of the forces as it rose to the surface and impacted the action of the Peloponnesian War.*

In what follows, it will be instructive to focus on two further ideas of Thucydides, both because they play particularly important parts in his account of the war and because they help to demonstrate the subtlety with which Thucydides treats most of the ideas he presents in his pages. The first of these is self-interest; the second is the unequal relationship that exists between different groups of peoples and states (that is, the strong and the weak).

Exploring the Ideas

Throughout his text, Thucydides presents competing ideas of what it means to act in one's self-interest. He contrasts narrow notions, or those that seem only to be about the here and now, with broader notions that look to the long term or to the wider interest of the society.

In the section known as the Melian dialogue,* for instance, we see the Athenians justify their decision to conquer the neutral Melian people with the claim that it was in their immediate self-interest to do so. The Athenians state boldly "we are here for the benefit of our empire," and they refuse to allow the idea of justice to limit their pursuit of gain. Against this, however, the Melians claim that it is in the Athenians' long-term self-interest to maintain the norms of justice. If they do not, the Melians say, "in the event of your downfall your retribution will be proportionately severe just because of the example you have set others."[1]

To the frustration of many readers, Thucydides does not provide clear approval for the position of either the Melians or the Athenians. He does not tell the reader which conception of interest is better or right. Rather, Thucydides is far more interested in understanding why individuals were motivated by one concept of self-interest rather than the other, and less interested in passing judgment on them for doing so.

In his analysis of plague, for instance, he describes how the sudden risk of immediate, indiscriminate death changed the way the Athenians identified what was good for them: "Whatever gave immediate pleasure or in any way facilitated it became the standard of what was good and useful. Neither fear of the gods nor law of man was any restraint: they judged it made no difference whether or not they showed them respect, seeing that everyone died just the same; on the contrary, no one expected to live long enough to go on trial and pay the penalty."[2]

Thucydides appears to accept that the strong have always ruled over the weak, as he builds this idea into his model of supposed Greek pre-history.[3] However, it is a deeply divisive issue in his text whether this rule is justified, and whether, or to what extent, the strong are obligated to treat the weak justly. Again, the most famous place we see this debate is in the Melian dialogue, where the Athenians assert that "judgments about justice are relevant only between those with an equal power to enforce it." They further suggest that, because the strong have always ruled over the weak, they are justified in doing so. The Melians counter by insisting that justice is important exactly because it protects the weak from the strong.[4]

Overlooked

Scholarship into Thucydides is as old as scholarship itself, and there are few parts of his text that have not been analyzed and discussed at some point.

The sheer complexity and richness of his text presents certain problems for the study of Thucydides today, however. Most immediately, it encourages disagreement over basic questions of interpreting Thucydides' thought. But it also presents a more specific problem in the modern study of Thucydides' text, having to do with the division of labor among scholars. This text does not easily fit into any single one of our present academic fields. Rather, it is pertinent to a number of them: history, political theory, social science, literature. This presents a problem for scholars, who frequently have trouble going beyond the boundaries of their discipline when studying the text.

Thucydides' approach to the Peloponnesian War is interdisciplinary, then, while scholars tend to work in one discipline, making it hard for them to do justice to the full complexity of the text.

Political theorists tend to study Thucydides' political thought; ancient historians study the accuracy of Thucydides' account; literature scholars study his narrative techniques; and so on. The unfortunate result is a discussion over Thucydides in the scholarly books and journals that can vary widely across disciplinary lines, with each distinct discipline and sub-discipline largely overlooking the conversations that the others are having.

NOTES

1   *Thucydides: The War of the Peloponnesians and the Athenians*, ed. and trans. Jeremy Mynott (Cambridge: Cambridge University Press, 2013), 380–1 [5.90–5.98].

2   *Thucydides: The War of the Peloponnesians and the Athenians*, 122 [2.53.3–4].

3   1.2–19.

4   *Thucydides: The War of the Peloponnesians and the Athenians*, 379–80 [5.89–90].

MODULE 7
ACHIEVEMENT

KEY POINTS

- Thucydides aimed to write a text that would be "useful" to future readers. Although his *History* has been widely cited since the beginning of the Renaissance* (the period, beginning in the fourteenth century, when European arts were reinvigorated by a turn towards the classics), its central message has been interpreted in opposing ways.

- It looks like Thucydides' immediate impact on Greek culture was very limited. He starts being seen as a key thinker only several centuries later, when the center of Mediterranean power moved from Greece to Rome.

- Later thinkers have turned to Thucydides as an ancient inspiration and authority for their ideas.

Assessing the Argument

In writing his *History of the Peloponnesian War*, Thucydides was hoping that such an accurate account would be thought "useful" by later generations, and a "possession for all time."[1] In some ways, Thucydides' achievement of this goal looks to be easy to measure. Western intellectuals have indeed used Thucydides' *History of the Peloponnesian War* widely for inspiration and to justify their own ideas since the Renaissance. If any work has a claim to being a possession for all time, Thucydides' might.

Even so, many scholars wish to know whether the text has in fact been useful in the way that Thucydides hoped it would be. The answer hangs on the question of "What exactly does Thucydides mean by 'useful'?" There have been mainly two different answers from scholars.

> ❝ Now to Thucydides the supreme requisite of a politician is his *prognôsis*—his ability to foresee—and the *History* itself is, in essence, a manual for future statesmen, instructing them in the outcome of conditions destined to be repeated. ❞
>
> John H. Finley, Jr., *Thucydides*

Some argue that by "useful," Thucydides meant that his work revealed certain universal truths about political life—natural laws, we might say—that individuals could understand and then use to shape historical developments as they wanted. According to this approach, Thucydides' text is considered to be "a manual for future statesmen," as the American classicist John H. Finley, Jr.* famously wrote, and should be read like a textbook that promised to unlock the secrets of political life.[2] Although this approach is commonly linked with the positivist historiographers* of the nineteenth and twentieth centuries, it has had forceful supporters from other academic traditions as well.[3]

In opposition to the optimistic reading of Thucydides is the pessimistic reading,[4] according to which Thucydides believed that historical developments are outside of human control. Subscribers to this view believe that Thucydides felt that no matter how hard humans tried or studied, they would never be able to change the unending patterns of political life; Thucydides did not expect his future readers to realize any greater control over their political environment than the men of his day, these scholars argue, even once they understood the knowledge that he had to offer. Rather, at the heart of Thucydides' wisdom is thought to be the lesson that even accurate knowledge about the historical process is not enough to bring about historical change.

If we accept the optimistic reading, it would seem Thucydides has not achieved his aim of being useful despite the frequent and varied use his book was put to by later thinkers. The problems of political life have not yet been solved, either by a reading of Thucydides or otherwise. Likewise, however, Thucydides has been equally unsuccessful according to the pessimistic reading. To the extent that we continue to try to solve political problems, and indeed believe that we can solve these problems by applying new ideas and theories, the pessimists' Thucydides has also failed in his aim.

Achievement in Context

There is actually very little that we can say for certain about the exact environment in which Thucydides' text was made public and the immediate reaction to it. In part this is because we have so little evidence from the period in general. But most of all, this is because Thucydides is never directly mentioned in any of the works that we might look to in attempting to provide context for his work.

It is clear that Thucydides wrote some parts of his text after the war's end in 404 B.C.E., and thus we know that he lived at least until then. However, we do not know at which point after this he died; whether he ever made it back to Athens; whether he wrote all of the text after the war's end or just pieces of it; or whether he made the text public before he died. In the other texts we have from the period, there is a notable silence surrounding Thucydides. Neither of the influential philosophers Plato* or Aristotle* mention him in their works, for instance, and only the historical writer Xenophon* suggests a clear awareness of his text—and in doing so does not mention Thucydides' name.

It was not until a few centuries later, when the center of power and culture in the Mediterranean had shifted to Rome, that Thucydides was finally identified as a central intellectual figure of fifth-century Athens.

Limitations

As recent scholarly work on the reception of Thucydides' text has shown, he has been read and cited with surprising regularity since the Renaissance, and he has occupied an unusually high position of intellectual authority across a number of European and world cultures.[5]

Moreover, these studies often highlight the extraordinary fact that Thucydides' text has been held up by opposing political programs, each claiming the text as a source of support. In the late Renaissance, for instance, he was seen as both a monarchist and a civic republican; in the Enlightenment* as both a supporter and critic of democracy. In this manner, Thucydides has remained the focus of constant debate in the Western intellectual tradition, and these debates in themselves are an important part of that tradition.[6] In other words, to be a member of the Western political tradition is, in part, to argue over interpretations of Thucydides.

But the Athenian has also impacted the Western tradition more indirectly as a key influence on figures such as the British philosopher Thomas Hobbes,* author of the highly influential work of political theory *Leviathan*, and the nineteenth-century philosopher Friedrich Nietzsche.* Both went on to rewrite the Western intellectual tradition in their own ways; Hobbes, for instance, famously called Thucydides the "most politic historian that ever writ,"[7] and the philosopher David Hume,* another giant of the Western tradition, wrote in 1742, "The first page of Thucydides is, in my opinion, the commencement of real history."[8]

NOTES

1 Thucydides, *The War of the Peloponnesians and the Athenians*, ed. and trans. Jeremy Mynott (Cambridge: Cambridge University Press, 2013), 15–16 [1.22.4].

2 John H. Finley, Jr., *Thucydides* (Cambridge, MA: Harvard University Press, 1942), 50.

3   For an excellent discussion of this position, see Hans-Peter Stahl,
    Thucydides: Man's Place in History (Swansea: Classical Press of Wales,
    2003 [1966]), 13–30.

4   For the seminal statements of this interpretive tradition, see Stahl,
    Thucydides, 1–10; and Adam Parry, "Thucydides' Historical Perspective,"
    Yale Classical Studies 22 (1971): 47–61.

5   See the collection of essays in Katherine Harloe and Neville Morley,
    eds., *Thucydides and the Modern World: Reception, Reinterpretation and
    Influence from the Renaissance to the Present* (Cambridge: Cambridge
    University Press, 2012).

6   Kinch Hoekstra, "Thucydides and the Bellicose Beginnings of Modern
    Political Theory," in Harloe and Morley, eds., *Thucydides*, 26, n. 4.

7   Thomas Hobbes, *The English Works of Thomas Hobbes of Malmesbury*, ed.
    Sir William Molesworth (London: John Bohn, 1966), viii.

8   David Hume, "On the Populousness of Ancient Nations," in *Essays: Moral,
    Political, and Literary* (Indianapolis, IN: Liberty Fund, 1985 [1742]), 422.

MODULE 8
PLACE IN THE AUTHOR'S WORK

KEY POINTS

- Thucydides' *History of the Peloponnesian War* appears to be his life's work and the only book he produced.
- Scholars have long argued over whether Thucydides wrote his text after the end of the war, or in large chunks at different times during the long conflict.
- Since the rebirth of interest in the work during the Renaissance,* it has come to be regarded as a key text for Western history, philosophy, and political science.

Positioning

As far as we know, Thucydides' *History of the Peloponnesian War* is the only work that he wrote. He appears to have devoted most of his mature life to its completion.

Thucydides tells the reader that he began this project at the outbreak of the Peloponnesian War* in 431 B.C.E. "in the expectation that this would be a great war and more worthy of account than any previous one."[1] Later, he adds, "I lived through the whole [of the war] when I was of an age to appreciate what was going on and could apply my mind to an exact understanding of things."[2] Based on this comment, and others like it, it is clear that Thucydides lived to see the end of the war, and he was apparently still at work on his account after it was over. This suggests that Thucydides was at work on his text about the war for at least 27 years, from 431 to (at least) 404 B.C.E.

We do not know how much longer after the war's end Thucydides remained alive, but the generally held belief is that it was less than a decade, and it may have been just a year or two. Whether he lived just a

> **❝** I lived through the whole of [the war] when I
> was of an age to appreciate what was going on and
> could apply my mind to an exact understanding of
> things. It so turned out that I was banished from my
> own country for twenty years after the Amphipolis
> campaign and thus had the time to study matters more
> closely; and as consequence of my exile I had access to
> activities on both sides. **❞**
>
> Thucydides, *History of the Peloponnesian War*

few years or a full decade is important for understanding how much of
the text could have been written after the war's conclusion.

Integration

Classical scholars have long been concerned with questions of when
and how Thucydides wrote the text.[3] The "Thucydides Question," as
this is known, has been answered in a number of different ways over
the last century.

Some scholars argue that the text was written all at once after the
war ended, and that Thucydides spent his time during the war
gathering facts and taking notes, not writing the final draft. Others
argue that significant chunks of the text that we have were written at
different times throughout the war and later stitched together into the
work that we know. These positions have often been called the
"unitarian"* and the "separatist"* readings of Thucydides' text.

Despite much debate in the early twentieth century, most of
which was in German, it is widely agreed now that we do not have
enough evidence to support either option—it can not be convincingly
demonstrated that the work was written at one time, nor that there are
different, identifiable parts of the work written in different periods.

In part because of this uncertainty, the "Thucydides Question" no longer concerns scholars with the same force as it did a century ago. Most scholars have now given up looking for identifiable sections written at different times, and they have become rather agnostic (admitting that they do not know) about the issue in general. Largely for practical reasons, most scholars now approach the text from a unitarian reading, viewing it as a single finished product.

Significance

As the only text that we have from Thucydides, his account of the Peloponnesian War tells us everything we are able to know about his thinking and nearly everything we are able to know about his life. It was this text that defined his life and continues to define the intellectual mark he left behind. Since the rebirth of interest in Thucydides' text in the Renaissance, many intellectuals have been eager to mine its wisdom and to claim its author as a sponsor for their particular political program.

Perhaps the most widely known modern tradition to claim Thucydides as a significant forefather is international relations realism.* Alongside the Italian political theorist Niccolò Machiavelli* and the English political philosopher Thomas Hobbes,* international relations realists have identified Thucydides as an ancient source for their vision; they see dealings among nations as anarchic, amoral, and guided by the self-interest of individual countries. In the last 30 years or so, however, this reading of Thucydides as an early international relations realist has come under heavy criticism by scholars in classics and political science. The increasingly dominant opinion now is that Thucydides was an early critic of the realist political approach, not its first champion.

Nevertheless, there is good reason to be cautious about assuming that Thucydides' political ideas hold direct relevance for the political divisions and programs of our day.

NOTES

1   Thucydides, *The War of the Peloponnesians and the Athenians*, ed. and trans. Jeremy Mynott (Cambridge: Cambridge University Press, 2013), 3 [1.1.1].

2   Thucydides, *The War of the Peloponnesians and the Athenians*, 339 [5.26.5].

3   For an overview, see Simon Hornblower, "Introduction: The Dates and Stages of Composition of 5.25–8.109," in *A Commentary on Thucydides*, vol. 3, bks. 5.25–8.109 (Oxford: Oxford University Press, 2010), 1–4.

SECTION 3
IMPACT

MODULE 9
THE FIRST RESPONSES

KEY POINTS

- There is a surprising silence surrounding Thucydides' text in the fourth century B.C.E.; the historian Xenophon* is the only scholar to mention him directly.

- We have no record of how the book was received at the time. The unfinished state of the final chapter suggests Thucydides could have died before making it public.

- It remains a mystery why this work, now recognized as a classic, apparently got very little attention in its day.

Criticism

There is reason to believe that some of Thucydides' contemporaries immediately recognized his *History of the Peloponnesian War* as an important work. Xenephon's history *Hellenica*, for instance, shows clear knowledge and respect for the text, picking up where Thucydides' narration of the Peloponnesian War* breaks off in 411 B.C.E.[1] Beyond Xenophon, however, we find that the Greek literary tradition is silent on what Thucydides intended to be a "possession for all time."[2] Most noticeably, his name is entirely absent in the works of Plato* and Aristotle* for reasons that are not entirely clear.

The absence of Thucydides in Aristotle's *Poetics* is most puzzling; in this work, Aristotle turns his attention towards the definition of history as a genre, which he contrasts with that of poetry.[3] Aristotle's argument, which directly names Herodotus,* is about a distinction between recounting particular facts (history) and demonstrating general truths (philosophy or poetry). History, Aristotle argues, recounts what was actually said or done, whereas "poetry" tells of what is likely or

> ❝ The difference between the historian and the
> poet is not that between using verse or prose ...
> No, the difference is this: that the one relates actual
> events, the other the kinds of things that might occur.
> Consequently, poetry is more philosophical and more
> elevated than history, since poetry relates more of the
> universal, while history relates particulars. ❞
>
> Aristotle, *Poetics*

necessary for an individual to do in a particular situation. Thucydides' account, however, was an attempt to explain particular facts in the context of general truths. Such a work does not fit into Aristotle's framework, suggesting that the philosopher was either unaware of the *History* or sought to redescribe historical inquiry in such a way that Thucydides could play no part in it.

Looking to the works of Plato, there are two dialogues in which it seems possible that Thucydides is being referred to, even if he is never mentioned by name. The first of these is Plato's text *Menexenus*, a dialogue between Plato's former teacher Socrates* and a man called Menexenus. In it, Plato offers a sort of parody of Pericles' funeral oration*—the sequence in Thucydides' *History* in which the Athenian leader Pericles gives a speech on the Athenian war dead.

The second of these is Plato's text *Gorgias*. In it, Socrates faces off with an Athenian politician named Callicles who voices extreme, amoral arguments similar to those found in the speeches of some of the figures that Thucydides includes in his book.[4] What is more, Socrates makes an extensive attack on Pericles as a democratic leader, suggesting that he "made the Athenians lazy, cowardly, babbling, and money lovers."[5] In so doing, Socrates makes no distinction between Pericles' style of political rhetoric and that of the politicians who came after him. Socrates does, however, make a contrast between the philosopher and the politician; for him, the former speaks the truth while the latter speaks only for gain.

As such a distinction plays a central role in Thucydides' analysis of Athens, we can see that the texts are in clear confrontation with each other. Many, indeed, have been encouraged to see Plato and Thucydides as fierce opponents of one another.[6] Nevertheless, we should be cautious in concluding that Plato was responding to Thucydides directly in either of his works. He does not anywhere say that he was, and it remains very possible that the two authors were independently responding to a common culture, not to each other. In this culture, references to Pericles' funeral oration, his legacy, and the legitimacy of realist political discourse would have been the subject of debate for many—not just Thucydides and Plato.

Responses

If it were made public in its own day, it is easy to imagine that Thucydides' work was both controversial and deeply admired. It was incredibly ambitious in its aims, and it offered a perspective on politics that was radical and new.

In terms of the immediate reception of his book, however, all we are able to do is to imagine. If Thucydides' text did cause an immediate stir among the Greek intellectual world of the fourth century B.C.E., we have no record of it. Likewise, we do not have any evidence to suggest how Thucydides responded, or whether he even had a chance to respond.

Based on the incomplete state of the final chapter, Book VIII, many scholars believe that Thucydides died while still at work on his text, thus never living to see the text made public. If this were the case, it is possible that he died without ever knowing how his life's work would be received. However, this is not the only possible reason for Thucydides' text being incomplete. It is possible, for instance, that there once was a complete manuscript that had its final books removed for political reasons at some point. Or, it is possible that Thucydides simply lost interest in documenting the final years of the war, focusing instead on polishing his account of the war's first 20 years.

Conflict and Consensus

Be that as it may, we can nevertheless speculate about how Thucydides wrote the text that comes down to us and whether or not he had a chance to incorporate criticisms into his writing before he died. It seems certain that some parts of this text were written after the end of the Peloponnesian War in 404 B.C.E., but this could suggest either that the whole of the text was written at this point or that these passages were later added to an already existing text.

These are the two opposing positions of the unitarian* and separatist* readings of Thucydides. If we follow this latter, "separatist," possibility further, we can imagine that Thucydides first wrote his accounts of the early years of the war and the phase of the war known as the Sicilian Expedition* soon after these events concluded in 413 B.C.E.

In that case he would have had lots of opportunity to show these works-in-progress to friends and other potential critics (indeed, we might wonder if it were possible for someone to work on a project for so long and *not* show it to anyone). We can also expect that Thucydides would have been routinely checking his text against the experiences of every new person he met, constantly seeking potential critics of his account in this way. All of that said, it is important to underline that this is mere speculation. There is almost nothing we can state for certain about when or where Thucydides wrote different parts of his final text, or who read it and responded to it.

NOTES

1   The continuity of the two stories seems to be emphasized by Xenophon
    in the first phrase of his work, *meta de tauta*, or "after these things." This
    was a conventional Greek formula for beginning a new episode in a larger
    chronological series, meaning that Xenophon seems to be clearly indicating
    that he is continuing something, not starting fresh. See Xenophon,
    Hellenica 1.1.1.

2   Thucydides, *The War of the Peloponnesians and the Athenians*, ed. and
    trans. Jeremy Mynott (Cambridge: Cambridge University Press, 2013), 16
    [1.22.4].

3   Aristotle, *Poetics* 1451b.

4   Plato, *Gorgias, Menexenus, Protagoras*, ed. M. Schofield, trans. T. Griffith
    (Cambridge: Cambridge University Press, 2010).

5   Plato, *Gorgias*, trans. J. Nichols, Jr. (Ithaca, NY: Cornell University Press,
    1998), 115.

6   See, for instance, Raymond Geuss, "Thucydides, Nietzsche, and Williams,"
    in *Outside Ethics* (Princeton, NJ: Princeton University Press, 2005), 219.

MODULE 10
THE EVOLVING DEBATE

KEY POINTS

- Thucydides' text has remained an important work since its reemergence into European culture in the Renaissance.*

- Thucydides' text has long been associated with the schools of political realism* (founded on the assumption that nations act in an amoral fashion out of sheer self-interest) and objective historiography* (an approach to writing history that focuses on the impartial documentation of individual facts).

- Since the end of the Cold War,* critics of realism and objective historiography have reclaimed Thucydides. His insistence on the need for accurate facts, however, makes him a key influence for all modern scholars.

Uses and Problems

Thucydides was already considered an authority on political matters in Roman times, thanks to his *History of the Peloponnesian War,* and in Western intellectual circles he has maintained this reputation since the sixteenth century.

The text reappeared in Europe from the city of Byzantium (what is today Istanbul) in the early fifteenth century, by way of Italy; its reception was restrained, however, by the fact that few people could read ancient Greek. Soon, however, in 1452, the *History* was translated into Latin, then French in 1527, and English in 1550.[1] By the sixteenth century, Thucydides had entered into the discussions of both European politics and political theory.

> 66 The name of Thucydides has the power to persuade, even or especially to persuade those with little or no direct knowledge of his work, and even when that name is invoked to support positions with no obvious connection to anything that Thucydides himself ever wrote. 99
>
> Katherine Harloe and Neville Morley, "Introduction: The Modern Reception of Thucydides"

Since his return in the fifteenth century, Thucydides has been read as an ally for all sorts of political and intellectual positions. In the twenty-first century, Thucydides' readers continue to disagree widely over what he is saying, and wider cultural battles are fought in part through competing interpretations of the text. In classics, for instance, supporters of objective and subjective historiography* (approaches to writing history that disagree on the extent to which the record is distorted by the biases of the historian) have both read Thucydides as being on their side.[2]

In political science, realists* (those who subscribe to the view that international relations are based on a somewhat ruthless pragmatism) and constructivists* (those who put a weight on the importance of conventions, norms, and other socially constructed facts) argue for both a realist and a constructivist Thucydides.[3]

Regardless of their position, scholars have often turned to Thucydides for support.

Schools of Thought

The most politically important school of thought to hold Thucydides up as its founder is international relations realism. Beginning with the start of the Cold War in the 1940s (a period of great political tension largely driven by the United States and the Soviet Union), realism emerged as a leading force in the academic study of international relations in the English-speaking world, led by scholars such as E. H. Carr,* Hans Morgenthau,* Robert Gilpin,* and Kenneth Waltz.*

Though these thinkers differed somewhat in approach and doctrine, realists in general argued that the international order was anarchic and filled with self-interested states. Therefore, they argued that successful policy must be based on self-interest and security, not moral rightness. Practically speaking, realism is often considered a hostile and aggressive political theory, called on to justify the preemptive use of military force and other actions of dubious morality when it is in a state's interest to do so.

Realists have regularly pointed to Thucydides as an ancient source and authority for their ideas, and for most of the twentieth century they succeeded in dominating the discussion over his text in political science. Moreover, the realists succeeded in focusing discussion on passages such as the section known as the Melian dialogue,* which were taken as particularly favorable to the realist cause.

One political theorist recently wrote, for instance, "The Thucydides who has been bowed (or at least nodded) to in the academic field of 'international relations' for the past seventy-five years is Thucydides the Realist. He is the clear-eyed theorist of power and interest, the debunker of moral illusions. His Melian dialogue, it is said, lays bare the true nature of international politics."[4]

In Current Scholarship

In the period following the Cold War, realism has lost its hold over international relations scholars, and the realist reading of Thucydides has lost many of its admirers. Scholars have criticized the realist reading of Thucydides for failing to differentiate between Thucydides the author on the one hand, and the speakers that he depicts on the other; as a result, the critics claim, realists failed to see that Thucydides was, at least in part, a critic of the views that the realists cite for authority.[5]

In turn, competing schools of thought in international relations theory have tried to take Thucydides from the realists and claim him for their own. Most noticeably, this has been done by the constructivists, who argue for an interpretation of Thucydides that brings him closer to their own philosophical beliefs.[6] One outspoken promoter of the constructivist Thucydides, for instance, has written, "If there is an intended political message in Thucydides, it is that secure and prosperous societies depend on conventions, and they must be restored and maintained by reason and language." In this way, this writer argues, Thucydides was the father of constructivism.[7]

Despite these debates, there are important but unrecognized ways in which all scholars in the Western tradition are working within the tradition Thucydides started. With his documentation and analysis of the Peloponnesian War,* he introduced an evidence-based approach to studying politics that continues to frame the Western idea of what serious intellectual practice is. Like Thucydides, scholars today tend to be skeptical of the idea of supernatural forces causing political developments, and focus on those forces that can be observed. Like Thucydides, today's scholars also tend to think that it is very important for their general theories about the world to be grounded in accurate facts. These are ideas that scholars draw on without even thinking about them, and some even do so without ever having read Thucydides.

Nevertheless, they can be traced back to Thucydides, who insisted on them at a time when it was not obvious that they were true.

NOTES

1   Katherine Harloe and Neville Morley, "Introduction: The Modern Reception of Thucydides," in *Thucydides and the Modern World: Reception, Reinterpretation and Influence from the Renaissance to the Present*, ed. Katherine Harloe and Neville Morley (Cambridge: Cambridge University Press, 2012), 4–5. Also, Kinch Hoekstra, "Thucydides and the Bellicose Beginnings of Modern Political Theory," in Harloe and Morley, eds., *Thucydides*, 25–6.

2   For an excellent and early discussion of the "objectivist" and "subjectivist" Thucydides, see W. R. Connor, "A Post-Modern Thucydides?," *Classical Journal* 72 (1977): 289–98.

3   For a discussion of the "realist" and "constructivist" Thucydides in modern political science, see Richard Ned Lebow, "International Relations and Thucydides," in Harloe and Morley, eds., *Thucydides*, 197–211.

4   Steven Forde, "Thucydides and 'Realism' among the Classics of International Relations," in Harloe and Morley, eds., *Thucydides*, 178.

5   For critiques of the realist Thucydides, see Gregory Crane, *Thucydides and the Ancient Simplicity: The Limits of Political Realism* (Berkeley, CA: University of California Press, 1998); Clifford Orwin, *The Humanity of Thucydides* (Princeton, NJ: Princeton University Press, 1994); and Josiah Ober, "Thucydides Theôrêtikos/Thucydides Histor: Realist Theory and the Challenge of History," in *War and Democracy: A Comparative Study of the Korean War and the Peloponnesian War*, ed. David McCann and Barry Strauss (London: Sharp, 2001), 273–306.

6   For the constructivist reading of Thucydides, see Richard Ned Lebow, "Thucydides the Constructivist," *American Political Science Review* 94 (2001): 574–600.

7   Lebow, "International Relations and Thucydides," 209.

MODULE 11
IMPACT AND INFLUENCE TODAY

KEY POINTS

- Thucydides' text remains the object of intense study in two academic fields: classics and political science.

- In recent years, there has been a dramatic shift away from reading Thucydides as a cold-hearted realist* and objectivist.* But interestingly, these recent critics have not rejected Thucydides; rather, they have reinterpreted his text's meaning.

- International relations realism has been a big loser from the post-Cold War* readings of Thucydides. Many scholars today feel the international relations realists quoted the ancient writer out of context to support their point of view.

Position

At present, two different academic fields—classics and political science—remain intensely interested in studying Thucydides' *History of the Peloponnesian War*. These two disciplines have produced different traditions of scholarly work by studying the text in very different ways. Classicists tend to focus on Thucydides' use of the ancient Greek language, his historical context, and his literary technique. The modern debate for them largely centers on what it means for Thucydides to be a historian. For political scientists, meanwhile, debate has focused on the extent to which he was a supporter or a critic of international relations realism.

Setting aside the question of Thucydides' realism temporarily, much of the recent scholarship on him by classicists has centered on understanding his "subjectivity"* (roughly, the way he understands

> ❝ The goal here is to root one's text or preferred
> discourse in a text or texts that have traditionally served
> to legitimize opposing texts or discourses ... The end of
> the Cold War provided the opportunity for non-realists
> to attempt to prise Thucydides loose from the realists'
> treasure chest. ❞
>
> Richard Ned Lebow, "International Relations and Thucydides"

and describes his experience according to his points of view), and the
way he uses certain storytelling techniques to incite emotion in his
reader. This "postmodern"* Thucydides, as he has been called, stems
from an attempt to correct the mid-twentieth-century reading of
Thucydides as an objective historian, or one whose sole mission and
worth was to impartially catalogue the facts.[1]

Against this tradition, modern classicists have focused on
Thucydides' own point of view and his literary cleverness in quietly
promoting it.[2] For these scholars, history is naturally subjective, as the
historian is always active and present in choosing which "facts" to
record for the reader, and in choosing how he or she will present
them. As a result, these scholars tend less often to ask the question,
"Was Thucydides right about what happened?" and more often to ask,
"What does Thucydides' presentation of what happened tell us about
his intentions and biases?"

Interaction

In both political science and classics, the current approach shows a
reaction against mid-twentieth-century readings. Current scholarly
writings reflect the wider divisions that have occurred in these
departments over this same period. In challenging the Thucydides of
the realist school of international relations and the Thucydides of the
objectivist school of historical analysis, scholars have also been

challenging the suitability of realism and objectivism for their own approach to the world, and for the future state of their disciplines. Debates over the interpretation of Thucydides have once again merged with wider debates over how we readers think about our own society.

What makes these recent attacks on the earlier views of a realist and objectivist Thucydides so interesting, however, is that they were not made in order to dismiss Thucydides as a thinker.[3] Rather, the recent scholars have tried to ground their critiques in a different reading of Thucydides' text, arguing that Thucydides was himself a critic of those approaches. Thus, rather than rejecting Thucydides, they have taken him over to their own cause, turning the text around on their opponents. As the constructivist* political theorist Richard Ned Lebow* states, "The end of the Cold War provided the opportunity for non-realists to attempt to prise Thucydides loose from the realists' treasure chest."[4]

The Continuing Debate

Though a few international relations realists continue to argue that Thucydides backs their views, for now it looks as if this reading of Thucydides is on the ropes. For many scholars, this is a welcome development. These scholars have long argued that the realists did not pay particularly close attention to the nuances of Thucydides' text, instead building their reading on a selection of convenient quotes taken out of context. Two experts on the ancient writer's reception have recently written, for instance, that is appears easy to dismiss the realist Thucydides based on "a naïve, partial and dehistoricised reading of a few isolated passages" in Thucydides' text.[5] This is a harsh judgment, and not one that these writers go on to fully accept, but it is a view that is increasingly held by contemporary scholars.

In the face of this criticism, there has not been a widespread and convincing response from the international relations realists. A few realists have carried on reading Thucydides according to the latest trends in international relations realism, more or less ignoring the critics of this approach.[6] But most others have simply grown quiet, and it is, so far, unclear whether there is anything more to say.

NOTES

1   W. R. Connor, "A Post-Modern Thucydides?," *Classical Journal* 72 (1977): 289–98.

2   For example, see W. R. Connor, *Thucydides* (Princeton, NJ: Princeton University Press, 1984); see also Tim Rood, *Thucydides: Narrative and Explanation* (Oxford: Oxford University Press, 1998).

3   For a work that might be considered an exception to this rule, see Marshall Sahlins, *Apologies to Thucydides: Understanding History as Culture and Vice Versa* (Chicago: University of Chicago Press, 2004).

4   Richard Ned Lebow, "International Relations and Thucydides," in *Thucydides and the Modern World: Reception, Reinterpretation and Influence from the Renaissance to the Present*, ed. Katherine Harloe and Neville Morley (Cambridge: Cambridge University Press, 2012), 202.

5   Katherine Harloe and Neville Morley, "Introduction: The Modern Reception of Thucydides," in Harloe and Morley, eds., *Thucydides*, 11–12.

6   For example, see Lawrence Tritle, "Thucydides and Power Politics," in *Brill's Thucydides*, ed. Antonios Rengakos and Antonis Tsakmakis (Leiden and Boston: Brill, 2006), 469–91.

MODULE 12
WHERE NEXT?

KEY POINTS

- Thucydides' text is likely to remain central to discussion for classicists and political scientists. And the prospect of more approaches to the text that simultaneously draw on different academic disciplines in the course of research is exciting.

- Increasingly, we might expect to find scholars interested in Thucydides' focus on what happens when politics in a democracy becomes more polarized and embittered. Likewise, his explorations of what it means for a democracy to lord over an empire may attract new attention.

- Thucydides' text remains a very useful tool for achieving a greater understanding of political life, both as it was in ancient Athens and in our own day.

Potential

Many scholars today believe that the realist* reading of Thucydides' *History of the Peloponnesian War* relies on a shallow and selective reading of his book. In reaction, some academics now say we should go so far as to stop reading Thucydides altogether, incapable as we are of understanding what he really meant.[1] Such voices, however, remain few, and there is no reason to believe that Thucydides' *History of the Peloponnesian War* will give up its unique grasp on the Western imagination any time soon. If the future is anything like the past, Thucydides will continue to be read for inspiration and cited for authority for all manner of different political opinions. Nevertheless, we can expect the particular ways in which Thucydides is read to develop considerably in the future.

> 66 [Thucydides] is constantly reread and reinterpreted in contemporary terms, and contemporary reality is interpreted in his terms. One might have expected that the advent of modernity ... would have made Thucydides' perspective seem redundant and placed his authority in question. In practice, it seems, modernity has appeared to be less different and unfamiliar, less of a break with the past, precisely because so many have continued to view the world through a Thucydidean lens. 99
>
> Katherine Harloe and Neville Morley, "Introduction: The Modern Reception of Thucydides"

The study of Thucydides is undergoing a period of change in both classics and political science, and this period is likely to be an exciting time of exploration, discovery, and reinterpretation. There are promising signs that this effort will benefit from the removal of some of the barriers between academic disciplines that have up to now held back the scholarly study of Thucydides.[2] Increasingly, scholars are aiming to produce interdisciplinary work (that is, work that draws on the methods, focus, and aims of different academic disciplines) and this movement is helping to bring political scientists, historians, and literary scholars into conversation with each other. We can expect that this will have good effects on the study of Thucydides, and that it will furnish readings that give us a better understanding of the ancient author and his text.

Future Directions

It is hard to say where future scholarship on Thucydides will go precisely. We can say with confidence, perhaps, only that it does not look like it will go away. It has recently been written, for instance, that

Thucydides "is constantly reread and reinterpreted in contemporary terms, and contemporary reality is interpreted in his terms."[3]

More concretely, in the immediate future we might predict an increased focus on Thucydides' analysis of situations where democratic politics fail to produce a unified citizen body or policy aimed at the collective good. Often overlooked by those with an international relations focus, Thucydides' analysis of the domestic situation in Athens throughout the Peloponnesian War* is as rich and complex as any found in the work. In this analysis, modern readers can find an investigation into the causes and consequences of political polarization in democratic governments that bears an eerie relevance to many twenty-first-century problems. As modern democratic citizens become more and more anxious about the ability of politicians to lead a democracy in an increasingly polarized and competitive situation, we might expect that scholars will increasingly turn their attention to this side of Thucydides' text. To some extent, this has already been happening in the work of the political scientists Richard Ned Lebow* and Josiah Ober,* but this is likely just the start.[4]

There are other aspects of Thucydides' text that we might also expect to receive increased attention in the years to come. Thucydides' discussions of the problems that typically arise in an empire run by a democracy, for instance, may seem an attractive focus for critics and proponents of US dominance and military actions in different parts of the world. Similarly, Thucydides' direct and indirect exploration of the psychological impacts of an overseas empire, both for the rulers and the ruled, may prove helpful in similar debates. Thucydides explores different possible motivations for having an empire, while resisting the tendency to reduce the discussion simply to moral failure and self-interest. Likewise, he voices arguments from both the ruling and the ruled, challenging the reader to see empire from both points of view without suggesting that one is obviously right and the other wrong.

Summary

Thucydides' *History* is unlike most other books that one will read. It is neither just history nor an abstract work of theory, but a piece of political inquiry that goes beyond these modern boundaries. At the same time, it is a piece of great literature, an epic in its own way. Throughout the work, Thucydides uses conflict and contradiction to challenge the reader towards a deeper understanding of politics. These conflicts expose the reader both to the variety of opinions and influences that make up political life, and the successes and the failures that they lead to.

Thucydides paints political life as a field of activity where many different factors have an impact. Much of the drama of Thucydides' text stems from the inability of its actors to ever fully account for or control all of the factors impacting their specific situation. Politics, for Thucydides, is never perfect, nor is it perfectly understandable, and it is often utterly devastating. It forces upon humans problems that can be managed for a time but never solved.

The reader of Thucydides sees that, for this reason, it is a deadly serious task to try to understand why politics works the way that it does. Likewise, the reader profits both from the thinking that Thucydides' words provoke and from comparing the vision of politics that Thucydides offers with the politics of his or her own day.

Thucydides does not answer all of our questions about political life, nor does he try. But he helps his reader to ask new, more interesting questions about the political world in which they live, and in this way we can certainly affirm that the text has achieved its goal of being "useful."

NOTES

1   For this claim, see David Welch, "Why International Relations Theorists Should Stop Reading Thucydides," *Review of International Studies* 29, no. 2 (2003): 301–19.

2   For two recent collections of work that indicate such a turn, see Edith
    Foster and Donald Lateiner, eds., *Thucydides and Herodotus* (Oxford:
    Oxford University Press, 2012); and Antonis Tsakmakis and M. Tamiolaki,
    eds.,*Thucydides between History and Literature. Trends in Classics –
    Supplementary Volumes*, bk. 17 (Berlin: De Gruyter, 2013).

3   Katherine Harloe and Neville Morley, "Introduction: The Modern Reception
    of Thucydides," in *Thucydides and the Modern World: Reception,
    Reinterpretation and Influence from the Renaissance to the Present*, ed.
    Katherine Harloe and Neville Morley (Cambridge: Cambridge University
    Press, 2012), 23–4.

4   For example, see Josiah Ober, *Political Dissent in Democratic Athens:
    Intellectual Critics of Popular Rule* (Princeton, NJ: Princeton University
    Press, 1998), chap. 2; see also Richard Ned Lebow, "Thucydides the
    Constructivist," *American Political Science Review* 94 (2001): 574–600.

GLOSSARY

GLOSSARY OF TERMS

Amphipolis: a strategically important city in north-central Greece. In 424 B.C.E., Thucydides was exiled from Athens after the Spartans gained control of this city.

Cold War: a largely non-violent period of great political tension between the United States and its allies and the Soviet Union, or USSR, and its allies that took place between 1945 and 1989.

Constructivism: a movement in international relations theories that emphasizes the importance of conventions, norms, and other socially constructed facts.

Enlightenment: a period of European history in which many traditional social and political ideas were challenged by rationalistic and skeptical thought. Though there is no definite start or end date, this period is generally associated with the seventeenth and eighteenth centuries.

Eponymous archon: an important office in Athens held for a year. In Athenian record, each year was named after the man that filled this office.

Hippocratic medical tradition: a group of medical parishioners that came together around the physician Hippocrates of Kos (c. 460–370 B.C.E.). Against traditional Greek practices, the Hippocratics viewed disease as a natural phenomenon, not as a supernatural one.

Melian dialogue: an episode at the end of Book 5 in Thucydides' history in which the Athenians try to convince the Melian people to capitulate and join their empire.

Neoconservatism: an important American political movement of the late twentieth and early twenty-first century committed to the aggressive, amoral pursuit of national interest. The neoconservative movement achieved its peak of political power during the presidency of George W. Bush.

Objective historiography: an approach to writing history that focuses on the impartial documentation of individual facts.

Peloponnesian War: a 27-year conflict (431–404 B.C.E.) between Athens, Sparta, and their respective allies in the fifth century B.C.E.

Pericles' funeral oration: a speech in Book 2 of Thucydides' text in which the Athenian leader Pericles offers a eulogy for the Athenian war dead by articulating an idealized picture of the Athenian way of life.

Persian Wars: A series of conflicts in the first half of the fifth century B.C.E. in which the Greeks repeatedly repulsed Persian invasions into their territory. This war produced many of the most famous battles of antiquity, including Marathon, Thermopylae, Salamis, and Plataea, and it was directly instrumental in the Athenians' acquisition of empire.

Positivist historiography: an approach to studying history that suggests that general historical laws can be discovered through the rigorous empirical study of historical facts.

Postmodern: a term that refers to a cultural movement of the twentieth century. In this context, it refers to the theoretical position that there is no certain, objective "truth" to be found in the analysis of historical events.

Realism: a highly influential school of thought in the field of international relations of the twentieth century, associated with Cold War politics. Those who subscribe to realist thought see relations between countries as anarchic, amoral, and self-interested. For them, countries should shape their policies to promote stability and their own security, rather than according to considerations of morality.

Renaissance: a historical period, roughly from the fourteenth to the seventeenth centuries, that marked the end of the medieval period, during which artists, writers, architects, and musicians reinvigorated European culture by turning towards ancient Rome and Greece.

Separatist reading: an approach to reading Thucydides' text that believes it was written in different stages over a period of time and that contradictions remain in the text as a result.

Sicilian Expedition: an expedition mounted by the Athenians in 415 B.C.E. to attack the island of Sicily with an enormous force with the intention of adding it to their empire. The Sicilian Expedition was a tremendous disaster for the Athenians, as few soldiers who were sent to Sicily ever returned.

Sophists: a group of traveling intellectuals practicing around the end of the fifth century B.C.E. They were known for their rationalism, skepticism, and willingness to go against standard opinion.

Subjective historiography: an approach to writing history that insists that all history is distorted to some degree by the biases of the historian, and therefore cannot be strictly objective.

Trojan War: a legendary war fought between the united Greeks and the Trojans over the abduction of Helen. This war is most famously depicted in Homer's *Iliad*.

Unitarian reading: an approach to reading Thucydides that reads the text as a finished literary product, not as a patchwork of pieces written at different times.

PEOPLE MENTIONED IN THE TEXT

Aristophanes (c. 445–385 B.C.E.) was an Athenian comedic playwright who was known for his biting satire of notable Athenian citizens. Amongst Aristophanes' most famous plays are his lampooning of Socrates in *The Clouds* and his satirical vision of female rule in *Lysistrata*.

Aristotle (384–322 B.C.E.) was a Greek polymath and philosopher who studied under Plato. Though he is now remembered primarily for his ethics and political theory, Aristotle also wrote important works on diverse subjects such as tragedy, rhetoric, and biology.

E. H. Carr (1892–1982) was an English historian, journalist, diplomat, and Woodrow Wilson Professor of International Politics at the University of Wales, Aberystwyth. He published books on international relations, Soviet Russia, and historiography.

Cimon (c. 510–450 B.C.E.) was a preeminent Athenian statesman and general in the early years of the empire. He was a member of the *Philaidae*, a leading aristocratic family that Thucydides is thought also to have belonged to.

Euripides (c. 480–406 B.C.E.) was the last of the three great Athenian tragedians. His most famous plays include *Medea* and *Bacchae*.

John H. Finley, Jr. (1904–95) was an American classicist and long-time professor at Harvard. He was a pioneer in the modern American study of Thucydides, perhaps most famous for his reading of Thucydides' text as a unified whole.

Robert Gilpin (b. 1930) is an American writer on international relations and political economy from the realist viewpoint. He is Professor Emeritus of Politics and International Affairs at the Woodrow Wilson School of Public and International Affairs at Princeton University.

Gorgias (c. 485–c. 380 B.C.E.) was an influential public speaker and teacher of rhetoric from the Sicilian city of Leontini. He was famous for a highly rhythmic and over-embellished style of speech.

Herodotus (c. 485–425 B.C.E.) is arguably the first historian of the Western tradition. In his *Histories*, he documents different competing accounts of the causes and events of the Persian Wars.

Hesiod (c. 700–800 B.C.E.) was a poet and farmer from the central Greek region of Boeotia. His most famous works include *Works and Days* and *Theogony*, the latter of which accounts for the rise of the Olympian gods and the ascension of Zeus to cosmic rule.

Thomas Hobbes (1588–1679) was an English philosopher and scientist. His most famous work is *Leviathan*, in which he argues for the crucial importance of a strong political sovereign.

Homer (c. 700–800 B.C.E.) was either a poet or a tradition of poets that wrote hugely influential epics. He is credited as the author of both the *Iliad* and the *Odyssey*.

David Hume (1711–76) was a Scottish philosopher, historian, and essayist. Like Thucydides, Hume was known for his extreme skepticism, his religious agnosticism, and his impartiality.

Irving Kristol (1920–2009) was an American journalist, editor, and founder of numerous political magazines. He is often considered to be a founding member of the neoconservative movement.

Richard Ned Lebow (b. 1942) is the James O. Freedman Presidential Professor Emeritus at Dartmouth College and the Professor of International Political Theory at King's College London. He is an outspoken member of the constructivist movement in international relations theory who frequently draws upon Thucydides in his work.

Niccolò Machiavelli (1469–1527) was a Florentine civil servant who wrote extensively on politics after his fall from power. He is best known for his work The Prince, in which an amoral approach to politics is encouraged.

Hans Morgenthau (1904–80) was a German American pioneer of the realist school of international relations. He was a professor at the University of Chicago, and later in New York.

Friedrich Nietzsche (1844–1900) was a widely influential German philologist and philosopher. Against the largely Christian leanings of his age, Nietzsche was known for looking up to a Greek ethic that privileged honor and power.

Josiah Ober (b. 1953) is a chaired professor of classics and political science at Stanford University. He is known for his penetrating investigation into the relationship between mass and elites in classical Athens.

Martin Ostwald (1922–2010) was a German American classicist who held positions at Swarthmore College and the University of Pennsylvania. Ostwald was an expert on archaic and classical Greek political and historical thought.

Pericles (c. 495–429 B.C.E.) was a preeminent Athenian statesman and general who led the city without interruption for nearly three decades (a period now known as Periclean Athens). As leader, Pericles presided over the apex of Athenian imperial power and encouraged the Athenians to enter into the Peloponnesian War.

Plato (c. 425–347 B.C.E.) was an Athenian philosopher and follower of Socrates, who often appears in his work as the main character. Plato's most famous Socratic dialogues are *Apology* and *Republic*.

Colin Powell (b. 1937) is a retired US general and civil servant. He served as both the chairman of the joint chiefs of staff under President George H.W. Bush and as secretary of state under President George W. Bush.

Protagoras (c. 490–c. 420 B.C.E.) was an influential sophist from the northern Greek city of Abdera. He was known for teaching the ability to argue on any side of a question and for his skepticism of supernatural forces.

Jacqueline de Romilly (1913–2010) was an influential French classicist and public intellectual, being the first woman to hold a position in the Collège de France and only the second woman in the Académie Française. She was famous for her readings of Thucydides' historical style and his discussion of Athenian imperialism.

Socrates (c. 469–399 B.C.E.) was an Athenian philosopher known for his critical conversations with his fellow citizens. Socrates never wrote any of his teachings down, but he has been immortalized in the works of his follower Plato.

Sophocles (c. 495–405 B.C.E.) was a widely successful Athenian tragedian who also served as general at least once. His most famous plays include *Antigone* and *Oedipus the King*.

Kenneth Waltz (1924–2013) was an American political scientist and founder of neorealism in international relations theory. He taught at the University of California, Berkeley, and Columbia University.

Xenophon (c. 430–354 B.C.E.) was an Athenian writer of histories, technical manuals, and Socratic dialogues. Like Thucydides, Xenophon was an accomplished soldier who was exiled from Athens relatively early in his life.

Xerxes (519–465 B.C.E.) was the king of Persia, 486–465 B.C.E. Under his command, Persian forces mounted an enormous attack on Greece where they were decisively defeated.

WORKS CITED

WORKS CITED

Canfora, L. "Biographical Obscurities and Problems of Composition." In *Brill's Companion to Thucydides*, edited by Antonios Rengakos and Antonis Tsakmakis, 3–32. Leiden: Brill, 2006.

Connor, W. R. "A Post-Modern Thucydides?" *Classical Journal* 72 (1977): 289–98.

— — —. *Thucydides*. Princeton, NJ: Princeton University Press, 1984.

Crane, Gregory. *Thucydides and the Ancient Simplicity: The Limits of Political Realism*. Berkeley, CA: University of California Press, 1998.

Farrar, Cynthia. *The Origins of Democratic Thinking: The Invention of Politics in Classical Athens*. Cambridge: Cambridge University Press, 1988.

Finley, John H., Jr. *Thucydides*. Cambridge, MA: Harvard University Press, 1942.

Forde, Steven. "Thucydides and 'Realism' among the Classics of International Relations." In *Thucydides and the Modern World: Reception, Reinterpretation and Influence from the Renaissance to the Present*, edited by Katherine Harloe and Neville Morley, 178–96. Cambridge: Cambridge University Press, 2012

Foster, Edith, and Donald Lateiner, eds. *Thucydides and Herodotus*. Oxford: Oxford University Press, 2012.

Geuss, Raymond. "Thucydides, Nietzsche, and Williams." In *Outside Ethics*, 219–33. Princeton, NJ: Princeton University Press, 2005.

Guthrie, W. K. C. *The Sophists*. Cambridge: Cambridge University Press, 1971.

Harloe, Katherine, and Neville Morley, eds. *Thucydides and the Modern World: Reception, Reinterpretation and Influence from the Renaissance to the Present*. Cambridge: Cambridge University Press, 2012.

Hawthorn, Geoffrey. *Thucydides on Politics: Back to the Present*. Cambridge: Cambridge University Press, 2014.

Hobbes, Thomas. *The English Works of Thomas Hobbes of Malmesbury*. Vol. 8, edited by Sir William Molesworth. London: John Bohn, 1966.

Hoekstra, Kinch. "Thucydides and the Bellicose Beginnings of Modern Political Theory." In *Thucydides and the Modern World: Reception, Reinterpretation and Influence from the Renaissance to the Present*, edited by Katherine Harloe and Neville Morley, 25–54. Cambridge: Cambridge University Press, 2012.

Hornblower, Simon. "Introduction: The Dates and Stages of Composition of 5.25–8.109." In *A Commentary on Thucydides*. Vol. 3. Bks. 5.25–8.109. Oxford: Oxford University Press, 2010.

Hume, David. "On the Populousness of Ancient Nations." In *Essays: Moral, Political, and Literary*, edited by Eugene F. Miller, 377–464. Indianapolis, IN: Liberty Fund, 1985 [1742].

Jouanna, Jacques. "Cause and Crisis in Historians and Medical Writers of the Classical Period." In *Hippocrates in Context: Papers Read at the 11th International Hippocrates Colloquium, University of Newcastle upon Tyne, August 27–31, 2002*, edited by Philip van der Eijk, 3–38. Leiden: Brill, 2005.

Kagan, Donald. *Thucydides: The Reinvention of History*. New York: Viking, 2009.

Kerferd, G. B. *The Sophistic Movement*. Cambridge: Cambridge University Press, 1981.

Kristol, Irving. "The Neoconservative Persuasion." *The Weekly Standard*, August 25, 2003. Accessed April 22, 2015. http://www.weeklystandard.com/Content/Public/Articles/000/000/ 003/000tzmlw.asp.

Kurke, Leslie. *Coins, Bodies, Games, and Gold: The Politics of Meaning in Archaic Greece*. Princeton, NJ: Princeton University Press, 1999.

———. "Charting the Poles of History: Herodotus and Thoukydides." In *Literature in the Greek and Roman Worlds: A New Perspective*, edited by Oliver Taplin, 133–55. Oxford: Oxford University Press, 2000.

Lebow, Richard Ned. "Thucydides the Constructivist." *American Political Science Review* 95 (2001): 547–60.

———. *The Tragic Vision of Politics: Ethics, Interests and Orders*. Cambridge: Cambridge University Press, 2003.

———. "International Relations and Thucydides." In *Thucydides and the Modern World: Reception, Reinterpretation and Influence from the Renaissance to the Present*, edited by Katherine Harloe and Neville Morley, 197–211. Cambridge: Cambridge University Press, 2012.

Lloyd, G. E. R. *The Revolutions of Wisdom: Studies in the Claims and Practice of Ancient Greek Science*. Berkeley, CA: University of California Press, 1987.

Maitland, Judith. "Marcellinus' Life of Thucydides: Criticism and Criteria in the Ancient Biographical Tradition." *Classical Quarterly* 46, no. 2 (1996): 538–58.

Nietzsche, Friedrich. *Twilight of the Idols with Antichrist and Ecce Homo*. Translated by A. Ludovici. Ware: Wordsworth Editions, 2007.

Ober, Josiah. *Political Dissent in Democratic Athens: Intellectual Critics of Popular Rule*. Princeton, NJ: Princeton University Press, 1998.

―――. "Thucydides Theôrêtikos/Thucydides Histor: Realist Theory and the Challenge of History." In *War and Democracy: A Comparative Study of the Korean War and the Peloponnesian War*, edited by David McCann and Barry Strauss, 273–306. London: Sharp, 2001.

Orwin, Clifford. *The Humanity of Thucydides*. Princeton, NJ: Princeton University Press, 1994.

Ostwald, Martin. *in Thucydides*. Atlanta, GA: Scholars Press, 1988.

Parry, Adam. "Thucydides' Historical Perspective." *Yale Classical Studies* 22 (1971): 47–61.

―――. Logos *and* Ergon *in Thucydides*. New York: Arno Press, 1981.

Plato. *Gorgias*. Edited by J. Nichols, Jr. Ithaca, NY: Cornell University Press, 1998.

―――. *Gorgias, Menexenus, Protagoras*. Edited by M. Schofield. Translated by T. Griffith. Cambridge: Cambridge University Press, 2010.

Romilly, Jacqueline de. *The Rise and Fall of States According to Greek Authors*. Ann Arbor, MI: University of Michigan Press, 1977.

―――. *The Mind of Thucydides*. Translated by Elizabeth Rawlings. Ithaca, NY: Cornell University Press, 2012 [1967].

Rood, Tim. *Thucydides: Narrative and Explanation*. Oxford: Oxford University Press, 1998.

Sahlins, Marshall. *Apologies to Thucydides: Understanding History as Culture and Vice Versa*. Chicago: University of Chicago Press, 2004.

Sharlin, Shifra. "Thucydides and the Powell Doctrine." *Raritan* 24, no. 1 (2004): 12–28.

Stahl, Hans-Peter. *Thucydides: Man's Place in History*. Swansea: Classical Press of Wales, 2003 [1966].

Thomas, Rosalind. *Herodotus in Context: Ethnography, Science and the Art of Persuasion*. Cambridge: Cambridge University Press, 2002.

―――. "Thucydides' Intellectual Milieu and the Plague." In *Brill's Companion to Thucydides*, edited by Antonios Rengakos and Antonis Tsakmakis, 87–108. Leiden: Brill, 2006.

Thucydides. *The War of the Peloponnesians and the Athenians*. Edited and translated by Jeremy Mynott. Cambridge: Cambridge University Press, 2013.

Tritle, Lawrence. "Thucydides and Power Politics." In *Brill's Companion to Thucydides*, edited by Antonios Rengakos and Antonios Tsakmakis, 469–91. Leiden: Brill, 2006.

Tsakmakis, Antonis, and Melina Tamiolaki, eds. *Thucydides between History and Literature. Trends in Classics – Supplementary Volumes.* Bk. 17. Berlin: De Gruyter, 2013.

Waterfield, Robin, trans. *The First Philosophers: The Presocratics and Sophists*. Oxford: Oxford University Press, 2000.

Welch. David. "Why International Relations Theorists Should Stop Reading Thucydides." *Review of International Studies* 29, no. 2 (2003): 301–19.

Williams, Bernard. *Truth and Truthfulness*. Princeton, NJ: Princeton University Press, 2003.

THE MACAT LIBRARY
BY DISCIPLINE

AFRICANA STUDIES

Chinua Achebe's *An Image of Africa: Racism in Conrad's Heart of Darkness*
W. E. B. Du Bois's *The Souls of Black Folk*
Zora Neale Huston's *Characteristics of Negro Expression*
Martin Luther King Jr's *Why We Can't Wait*
Toni Morrison's *Playing in the Dark: Whiteness in the American Literary Imagination*

ANTHROPOLOGY

Arjun Appadurai's *Modernity at Large: Cultural Dimensions of Globalisation*
Philippe Ariès's *Centuries of Childhood*
Franz Boas's *Race, Language and Culture*
Kim Chan & Renée Mauborgne's *Blue Ocean Strategy*
Jared Diamond's *Guns, Germs & Steel: the Fate of Human Societies*
Jared Diamond's *Collapse: How Societies Choose to Fail or Survive*
E. E. Evans-Pritchard's *Witchcraft, Oracles and Magic Among the Azande*
James Ferguson's *The Anti-Politics Machine*
Clifford Geertz's *The Interpretation of Cultures*
David Graeber's *Debt: the First 5000 Years*
Karen Ho's *Liquidated: An Ethnography of Wall Street*
Geert Hofstede's *Culture's Consequences: Comparing Values, Behaviors, Institutes and Organizations across Nations*
Claude Lévi-Strauss's *Structural Anthropology*
Jay Macleod's *Ain't No Makin' It: Aspirations and Attainment in a Low-Income Neighborhood*
Saba Mahmood's *The Politics of Piety: The Islamic Revival and the Feminist Subject*
Marcel Mauss's *The Gift*

BUSINESS

Jean Lave & Etienne Wenger's *Situated Learning*
Theodore Levitt's *Marketing Myopia*
Burton G. Malkiel's *A Random Walk Down Wall Street*
Douglas McGregor's *The Human Side of Enterprise*
Michael Porter's *Competitive Strategy: Creating and Sustaining Superior Performance*
John Kotter's *Leading Change*
C. K. Prahalad & Gary Hamel's *The Core Competence of the Corporation*

CRIMINOLOGY

Michelle Alexander's *The New Jim Crow: Mass Incarceration in the Age of Colorblindness*
Michael R. Gottfredson & Travis Hirschi's *A General Theory of Crime*
Richard Herrnstein & Charles A. Murray's *The Bell Curve: Intelligence and Class Structure in American Life*
Elizabeth Loftus's *Eyewitness Testimony*
Jay Macleod's *Ain't No Makin' It: Aspirations and Attainment in a Low-Income Neighborhood*
Philip Zimbardo's *The Lucifer Effect*

ECONOMICS

Janet Abu-Lughod's *Before European Hegemony*
Ha-Joon Chang's *Kicking Away the Ladder*
David Brion Davis's *The Problem of Slavery in the Age of Revolution*
Milton Friedman's *The Role of Monetary Policy*
Milton Friedman's *Capitalism and Freedom*
David Graeber's *Debt: the First 5000 Years*
Friedrich Hayek's *The Road to Serfdom*
Karen Ho's *Liquidated: An Ethnography of Wall Street*

John Maynard Keynes's *The General Theory of Employment, Interest and Money*
Charles P. Kindleberger's *Manias, Panics and Crashes*
Robert Lucas's *Why Doesn't Capital Flow from Rich to Poor Countries?*
Burton G. Malkiel's *A Random Walk Down Wall Street*
Thomas Robert Malthus's *An Essay on the Principle of Population*
Karl Marx's *Capital*
Thomas Piketty's *Capital in the Twenty-First Century*
Amartya Sen's *Development as Freedom*
Adam Smith's *The Wealth of Nations*
Nassim Nicholas Taleb's *The Black Swan: The Impact of the Highly Improbable*
Amos Tversky's & Daniel Kahneman's *Judgment under Uncertainty: Heuristics and Biases*
Mahbub Ul Haq's *Reflections on Human Development*
Max Weber's *The Protestant Ethic and the Spirit of Capitalism*

FEMINISM AND GENDER STUDIES

Judith Butler's *Gender Trouble*
Simone De Beauvoir's *The Second Sex*
Michel Foucault's *History of Sexuality*
Betty Friedan's *The Feminine Mystique*
Saba Mahmood's *The Politics of Piety: The Islamic Revival and the Feminist Subject*
Joan Wallach Scott's *Gender and the Politics of History*
Mary Wollstonecraft's *A Vindication of the Rights of Woman*
Virginia Woolf's *A Room of One's Own*

GEOGRAPHY

The Brundtland Report's *Our Common Future*
Rachel Carson's *Silent Spring*
Charles Darwin's *On the Origin of Species*
James Ferguson's *The Anti-Politics Machine*
Jane Jacobs's *The Death and Life of Great American Cities*
James Lovelock's *Gaia: A New Look at Life on Earth*
Amartya Sen's *Development as Freedom*
Mathis Wackernagel & William Rees's *Our Ecological Footprint*

HISTORY

Janet Abu-Lughod's *Before European Hegemony*
Benedict Anderson's *Imagined Communities*
Bernard Bailyn's *The Ideological Origins of the American Revolution*
Hanna Batatu's *The Old Social Classes And The Revolutionary Movements Of Iraq*
Christopher Browning's *Ordinary Men: Reserve Police Batallion 101 and the Final Solution in Poland*
Edmund Burke's *Reflections on the Revolution in France*
William Cronon's *Nature's Metropolis: Chicago And The Great West*
Alfred W. Crosby's *The Columbian Exchange*
Hamid Dabashi's *Iran: A People Interrupted*
David Brion Davis's *The Problem of Slavery in the Age of Revolution*
Nathalie Zemon Davis's *The Return of Martin Guerre*
Jared Diamond's *Guns, Germs & Steel: the Fate of Human Societies*
Frank Dikotter's *Mao's Great Famine*
John W Dower's *War Without Mercy: Race And Power In The Pacific War*
W. E. B. Du Bois's *The Souls of Black Folk*
Richard J. Evans's *In Defence of History*
Lucien Febvre's *The Problem of Unbelief in the 16th Century*
Sheila Fitzpatrick's *Everyday Stalinism*

The Macat Library By Discipline

Eric Foner's *Reconstruction: America's Unfinished Revolution, 1863-1877*
Michel Foucault's *Discipline and Punish*
Michel Foucault's *History of Sexuality*
Francis Fukuyama's *The End of History and the Last Man*
John Lewis Gaddis's *We Now Know: Rethinking Cold War History*
Ernest Gellner's *Nations and Nationalism*
Eugene Genovese's *Roll, Jordan, Roll: The World the Slaves Made*
Carlo Ginzburg's *The Night Battles*
Daniel Goldhagen's *Hitler's Willing Executioners*
Jack Goldstone's *Revolution and Rebellion in the Early Modern World*
Antonio Gramsci's *The Prison Notebooks*
Alexander Hamilton, John Jay & James Madison's *The Federalist Papers*
Christopher Hill's *The World Turned Upside Down*
Carole Hillenbrand's *The Crusades: Islamic Perspectives*
Thomas Hobbes's *Leviathan*
Eric Hobsbawm's *The Age Of Revolution*
John A. Hobson's *Imperialism: A Study*
Albert Hourani's *History of the Arab Peoples*
Samuel P. Huntington's *The Clash of Civilizations and the Remaking of World Order*
C. L. R. James's *The Black Jacobins*
Tony Judt's *Postwar: A History of Europe Since 1945*
Ernst Kantorowicz's *The King's Two Bodies: A Study in Medieval Political Theology*
Paul Kennedy's *The Rise and Fall of the Great Powers*
Ian Kershaw's *The "Hitler Myth": Image and Reality in the Third Reich*
John Maynard Keynes's *The General Theory of Employment, Interest and Money*
Charles P. Kindleberger's *Manias, Panics and Crashes*
Martin Luther King Jr's *Why We Can't Wait*
Henry Kissinger's *World Order: Reflections on the Character of Nations and the Course of History*
Thomas Kuhn's *The Structure of Scientific Revolutions*
Georges Lefebvre's *The Coming of the French Revolution*
John Locke's *Two Treatises of Government*
Niccolò Machiavelli's *The Prince*
Thomas Robert Malthus's *An Essay on the Principle of Population*
Mahmood Mamdani's *Citizen and Subject: Contemporary Africa And The Legacy Of Late Colonialism*
Karl Marx's *Capital*
Stanley Milgram's *Obedience to Authority*
John Stuart Mill's *On Liberty*
Thomas Paine's *Common Sense*
Thomas Paine's *Rights of Man*
Geoffrey Parker's *Global Crisis: War, Climate Change and Catastrophe in the Seventeenth Century*
Jonathan Riley-Smith's *The First Crusade and the Idea of Crusading*
Jean-Jacques Rousseau's *The Social Contract*
Joan Wallach Scott's *Gender and the Politics of History*
Theda Skocpol's *States and Social Revolutions*
Adam Smith's *The Wealth of Nations*
Timothy Snyder's *Bloodlands: Europe Between Hitler and Stalin*
Sun Tzu's *The Art of War*
Keith Thomas's *Religion and the Decline of Magic*
Thucydides's *The History of the Peloponnesian War*
Frederick Jackson Turner's *The Significance of the Frontier in American History*
Odd Arne Westad's *The Global Cold War: Third World Interventions And The Making Of Our Times*

LITERATURE

Chinua Achebe's *An Image of Africa: Racism in Conrad's Heart of Darkness*
Roland Barthes's *Mythologies*
Homi K. Bhabha's *The Location of Culture*
Judith Butler's *Gender Trouble*
Simone De Beauvoir's *The Second Sex*
Ferdinand De Saussure's *Course in General Linguistics*
T. S. Eliot's *The Sacred Wood: Essays on Poetry and Criticism*
Zora Neale Huston's *Characteristics of Negro Expression*
Toni Morrison's *Playing in the Dark: Whiteness in the American Literary Imagination*
Edward Said's *Orientalism*
Gayatri Chakravorty Spivak's *Can the Subaltern Speak?*
Mary Wollstonecraft's *A Vindication of the Rights of Women*
Virginia Woolf's *A Room of One's Own*

PHILOSOPHY

Elizabeth Anscombe's *Modern Moral Philosophy*
Hannah Arendt's *The Human Condition*
Aristotle's *Metaphysics*
Aristotle's *Nicomachean Ethics*
Edmund Gettier's *Is Justified True Belief Knowledge?*
Georg Wilhelm Friedrich Hegel's *Phenomenology of Spirit*
David Hume's *Dialogues Concerning Natural Religion*
David Hume's *The Enquiry for Human Understanding*
Immanuel Kant's *Religion within the Boundaries of Mere Reason*
Immanuel Kant's *Critique of Pure Reason*
Søren Kierkegaard's *The Sickness Unto Death*
Søren Kierkegaard's *Fear and Trembling*
C. S. Lewis's *The Abolition of Man*
Alasdair MacIntyre's *After Virtue*
Marcus Aurelius's *Meditations*
Friedrich Nietzsche's *On the Genealogy of Morality*
Friedrich Nietzsche's *Beyond Good and Evil*
Plato's *Republic*
Plato's *Symposium*
Jean-Jacques Rousseau's *The Social Contract*
Gilbert Ryle's *The Concept of Mind*
Baruch Spinoza's *Ethics*
Sun Tzu's *The Art of War*
Ludwig Wittgenstein's *Philosophical Investigations*

POLITICS

Benedict Anderson's *Imagined Communities*
Aristotle's *Politics*
Bernard Bailyn's *The Ideological Origins of the American Revolution*
Edmund Burke's *Reflections on the Revolution in France*
John C. Calhoun's *A Disquisition on Government*
Ha-Joon Chang's *Kicking Away the Ladder*
Hamid Dabashi's *Iran: A People Interrupted*
Hamid Dabashi's *Theology of Discontent: The Ideological Foundation of the Islamic Revolution in Iran*
Robert Dahl's *Democracy and its Critics*
Robert Dahl's *Who Governs?*
David Brion Davis's *The Problem of Slavery in the Age of Revolution*

The Macat Library By Discipline

Alexis De Tocqueville's *Democracy in America*
James Ferguson's *The Anti-Politics Machine*
Frank Dikotter's *Mao's Great Famine*
Sheila Fitzpatrick's *Everyday Stalinism*
Eric Foner's *Reconstruction: America's Unfinished Revolution, 1863-1877*
Milton Friedman's *Capitalism and Freedom*
Francis Fukuyama's *The End of History and the Last Man*
John Lewis Gaddis's *We Now Know: Rethinking Cold War History*
Ernest Gellner's *Nations and Nationalism*
David Graeber's *Debt: the First 5000 Years*
Antonio Gramsci's *The Prison Notebooks*
Alexander Hamilton, John Jay & James Madison's *The Federalist Papers*
Friedrich Hayek's *The Road to Serfdom*
Christopher Hill's *The World Turned Upside Down*
Thomas Hobbes's *Leviathan*
John A. Hobson's *Imperialism: A Study*
Samuel P. Huntington's *The Clash of Civilizations and the Remaking of World Order*
Tony Judt's *Postwar: A History of Europe Since 1945*
David C. Kang's *China Rising: Peace, Power and Order in East Asia*
Paul Kennedy's *The Rise and Fall of Great Powers*
Robert Keohane's *After Hegemony*
Martin Luther King Jr.'s *Why We Can't Wait*
Henry Kissinger's *World Order: Reflections on the Character of Nations and the Course of History*
John Locke's *Two Treatises of Government*
Niccolò Machiavelli's *The Prince*
Thomas Robert Malthus's *An Essay on the Principle of Population*
Mahmood Mamdani's *Citizen and Subject: Contemporary Africa And The Legacy Of
Late Colonialism*
Karl Marx's *Capital*
John Stuart Mill's *On Liberty*
John Stuart Mill's *Utilitarianism*
Hans Morgenthau's *Politics Among Nations*
Thomas Paine's *Common Sense*
Thomas Paine's *Rights of Man*
Thomas Piketty's *Capital in the Twenty-First Century*
Robert D. Putnam's *Bowling Alone*
John Rawls's *Theory of Justice*
Jean-Jacques Rousseau's *The Social Contract*
Theda Skocpol's *States and Social Revolutions*
Adam Smith's *The Wealth of Nations*
Sun Tzu's *The Art of War*
Henry David Thoreau's *Civil Disobedience*
Thucydides's *The History of the Peloponnesian War*
Kenneth Waltz's *Theory of International Politics*
Max Weber's *Politics as a Vocation*
Odd Arne Westad's *The Global Cold War: Third World Interventions And The Making Of Our Times*

POSTCOLONIAL STUDIES

Roland Barthes's *Mythologies*
Frantz Fanon's *Black Skin, White Masks*
Homi K. Bhabha's *The Location of Culture*
Gustavo Gutiérrez's *A Theology of Liberation*
Edward Said's *Orientalism*
Gayatri Chakravorty Spivak's *Can the Subaltern Speak?*

PSYCHOLOGY

Gordon Allport's *The Nature of Prejudice*
Alan Baddeley & Graham Hitch's *Aggression: A Social Learning Analysis*
Albert Bandura's *Aggression: A Social Learning Analysis*
Leon Festinger's *A Theory of Cognitive Dissonance*
Sigmund Freud's *The Interpretation of Dreams*
Betty Friedan's *The Feminine Mystique*
Michael R. Gottfredson & Travis Hirschi's *A General Theory of Crime*
Eric Hoffer's *The True Believer: Thoughts on the Nature of Mass Movements*
William James's *Principles of Psychology*
Elizabeth Loftus's *Eyewitness Testimony*
A. H. Maslow's *A Theory of Human Motivation*
Stanley Milgram's *Obedience to Authority*
Steven Pinker's *The Better Angels of Our Nature*
Oliver Sacks's *The Man Who Mistook His Wife For a Hat*
Richard Thaler & Cass Sunstein's *Nudge: Improving Decisions About Health, Wealth and Happiness*
Amos Tversky's *Judgment under Uncertainty: Heuristics and Biases*
Philip Zimbardo's *The Lucifer Effect*

SCIENCE

Rachel Carson's *Silent Spring*
William Cronon's *Nature's Metropolis: Chicago And The Great West*
Alfred W. Crosby's *The Columbian Exchange*
Charles Darwin's *On the Origin of Species*
Richard Dawkin's *The Selfish Gene*
Thomas Kuhn's *The Structure of Scientific Revolutions*
Geoffrey Parker's *Global Crisis: War, Climate Change and Catastrophe in the Seventeenth Century*
Mathis Wackernagel & William Rees's *Our Ecological Footprint*

SOCIOLOGY

Michelle Alexander's *The New Jim Crow: Mass Incarceration in the Age of Colorblindness*
Gordon Allport's *The Nature of Prejudice*
Albert Bandura's *Aggression: A Social Learning Analysis*
Hanna Batatu's *The Old Social Classes And The Revolutionary Movements Of Iraq*
Ha-Joon Chang's *Kicking Away the Ladder*
W. E. B. Du Bois's *The Souls of Black Folk*
Émile Durkheim's *On Suicide*
Frantz Fanon's *Black Skin, White Masks*
Frantz Fanon's *The Wretched of the Earth*
Eric Foner's *Reconstruction: America's Unfinished Revolution, 1863-1877*
Eugene Genovese's *Roll, Jordan, Roll: The World the Slaves Made*
Jack Goldstone's *Revolution and Rebellion in the Early Modern World*
Antonio Gramsci's *The Prison Notebooks*
Richard Herrnstein & Charles A Murray's *The Bell Curve: Intelligence and Class Structure in American Life*
Eric Hoffer's *The True Believer: Thoughts on the Nature of Mass Movements*
Jane Jacobs's *The Death and Life of Great American Cities*
Robert Lucas's *Why Doesn't Capital Flow from Rich to Poor Countries?*
Jay Macleod's *Ain't No Makin' It: Aspirations and Attainment in a Low Income Neighborhood*
Elaine May's *Homeward Bound: American Families in the Cold War Era*
Douglas McGregor's *The Human Side of Enterprise*
C. Wright Mills's *The Sociological Imagination*

Thomas Piketty's *Capital in the Twenty-First Century*
Robert D. Putman's *Bowling Alone*
David Riesman's *The Lonely Crowd: A Study of the Changing American Character*
Edward Said's *Orientalism*
Joan Wallach Scott's *Gender and the Politics of History*
Theda Skocpol's *States and Social Revolutions*
Max Weber's *The Protestant Ethic and the Spirit of Capitalism*

THEOLOGY

Augustine's *Confessions*
Benedict's *Rule of St Benedict*
Gustavo Gutiérrez's *A Theology of Liberation*
Carole Hillenbrand's *The Crusades: Islamic Perspectives*
David Hume's *Dialogues Concerning Natural Religion*
Immanuel Kant's *Religion within the Boundaries of Mere Reason*
Ernst Kantorowicz's *The King's Two Bodies: A Study in Medieval Political Theology*
Søren Kierkegaard's *The Sickness Unto Death*
C. S. Lewis's *The Abolition of Man*
Saba Mahmood's *The Politics of Piety: The Islamic Revival and the Feminist Subject*
Baruch Spinoza's *Ethics*
Keith Thomas's *Religion and the Decline of Magic*

COMING SOON

Chris Argyris's *The Individual and the Organisation*
Seyla Benhabib's *The Rights of Others*
Walter Benjamin's *The Work Of Art in the Age of Mechanical Reproduction*
John Berger's *Ways of Seeing*
Pierre Bourdieu's *Outline of a Theory of Practice*
Mary Douglas's *Purity and Danger*
Roland Dworkin's *Taking Rights Seriously*
James G. March's *Exploration and Exploitation in Organisational Learning*
Ikujiro Nonaka's *A Dynamic Theory of Organizational Knowledge Creation*
Griselda Pollock's *Vision and Difference*
Amartya Sen's *Inequality Re-Examined*
Susan Sontag's *On Photography*
Yasser Tabbaa's *The Transformation of Islamic Art*
Ludwig von Mises's *Theory of Money and Credit*

Printed in the United States
by Baker & Taylor Publisher Services